The Power of Emergent Curriculum:
Stories From Early Childhood Settings

Carol Anne Wien

In memory of Ann Yetman
extraordinary friend, artist, poet, teacher

The Power of Emergent Curriculum

Stories From Early Childhood Settings

Carol Anne Wien

National Association for the Education of Young Children
Washington, DC

National Association for the
Education of Young Children
1313 L Street NW, Suite 500
Washington, DC 20005-4101
202-232-8777 • 800-424-2460
www.naeyc.org

NAEYC Books

Chief Publishing Officer
Derry Koralek

Editor-in-Chief
Kathy Charner

Director of Creative Services
Edwin C. Malstrom

Managing Editor
Mary Jaffe

Senior Editor
Holly Bohart

Senior Graphic Designer
Malini Dominey

Associate Editor
Elizabeth Wegner

Editorial Assistant
Ryan Smith

Permissions

The excerpt on page 6 is from pages 5–6 in *Emergent Curriculum in the Primary Classroom: Interpreting the Reggio Emilia Approach in Schools*, by Carol Anne Wien, editor. 2008. New York: Teachers College Press. Reprinted with permission.

Photo Credits

Copyright © by: Julia Luckenbill: v (second from the top), 11 (top), 13, 16, 17, 18 (top and bottom), 19; New Canaan Nature Center: v (fourth from the top), 11 (bottom), 39; Karen Phillips: 41, 43, 46; Ellen B. Senisi: 45. The remaining photographs and children's art are courtesy of the authors.

Credits

Cover design: Edwin Malstrom

Contributing editors: Bry Pollack and Amy Shillady

Library of Congress Control Number: 2013947531
ISBN: 978-1-938113-02-4
NAEYC Item #181

Contents

Foreword

Amy Laura Dombro

Welcome to *The Power of Emergent Curriculum: Stories From Early Childhood Settings*, a book about intentional and responsive teaching. Seven of the ten chapters in the book were developed through a collaboration between the leadership and staff at Peter Green Hall Children's Centre in Halifax, Nova Scotia, Canada, and Carol Anne Wien, a wise writer, storyteller, professor in the Faculty of Education at York University in Toronto, Canada, and longtime friend of Peter Green Hall. The shared authorship of these pieces reflects the deep respect of these collaborators, who are learning together and realize that without all of their experiences and contributions, there would be no story to share about the life and learning of children and adults at Peter Green Hall.

Each of the stories that takes place at Peter Green Hall represents a point in time along an ongoing professional development journey as teachers at this early childhood setting learn about, create, and respond to emergent curriculum. It is a journey of ups and downs with bittersweet moments and moments of pride and joy as educators evolve from feeling hesitant and anxious to confident in their ability to embrace the content that emerges in the everyday life of an early childhood program.

Peter Green Hall serves children from infants to after-schoolers and their families. It is situated on the ground floor of a 14-story apartment building that houses graduate student families in Halifax. The families in the building come from all around the world. Many have children in the center; other children in the center come from the local community. The center thus serves a highly diverse population with both local and international roots (see the box "About the Peter Green Hall Children's Centre").

"It's not a pretty place," says Carol Anne. "It's surrounded by concrete and a chain-link fence." But take a closer look and you will see that though there may be fences on the outside, inside life is all about building connections and stretching thinking and learning to new places. You'll notice a welcoming sign and a garden lovingly tended on the north side of the building. You will see parents, sometimes wearing their bathrobes, bringing their children downstairs to "school," hanging out and talking with program staff.

When Barbara Bigelow took over as director of Peter Green Hall in 1990, the program was very traditional. In her efforts to make the program more developmentally appropriate, Barb reached out to the community to build connections that allowed her and the program to both contribute outside the center's walls and invite people in to be resources. Carol Anne was one who visited.

Under Barb's direction and with Carol Anne's support, the staff has been influenced by the ideas and practices of the Reggio Emilia experience, using them as points of departure for rethinking their own practices. Carol Anne writes: "Over time, the program has trans-

Chapter 4 "From Policing to Participation: Overturning the Rules and Creating Amiable Classrooms" occurred at three Hamilton, Ontario child care settings: McMaster Children's Centre, Templemead School, and Scott Park Children's Centre. Chapter 6 "The Visible Empathy of Infants and Toddlers" was undertaken by Valerie Quann as her master's research project in a lab school in a local Toronto university.

About the Peter Green Hall Children's Centre

Carol Anne Wien

Peter Green Hall Children's Centre in Halifax, Nova Scotia (Canada), is a nonprofit child care center owned by Dalhousie University for the children of students at five local universities and community colleges. The center is located on the ground floor of the 14-story Peter Green Hall apartment building, which provides housing for student families. The center serves a hundred or so children, birth through age 10. The families, who are culturally and economically diverse, include international students and students from the local community. The center staff care for and support the development and learning of infants through preschoolers and provide an after-school program for children ages 5–10.

Under the guidance of the director, Barbara Bigelow, the Reggio Emilia experience has influenced and inspired the center since 1996. "The Reggio Emilia approach is based in the municipal system of 46 centers for children from birth to age 6, owned and operated by the city of Reggio Emilia in northern Italy since the 1960s" (Wien 2008, 2). The Reggio experience emphasizes children's capability and resourcefulness, and has made an impact worldwide, ensuring children's views are more visible and their voices heard.

Peter Green Hall has re-created its own practices (inspired by practices and values of the Reggio Emilia experience) and supports staff in creating an emergent curriculum (Cadwell 2003; Edwards, Gandini, & Forman 2012). After more than a decade of transformation, the program has expanded from developmentally appropriate practice to emergent and Reggio-inspired early childhood practices with highly participatory structures and continuous collaboration among children, families, and teachers. The classroom environments and garden have evolved to build connections both to children's and teachers' interests and to the local community. The center supports children, teachers, and families in believing in their ideas and in their participation to realize those ideas in daily life. This sensibility promotes both democratic citizenship and the satisfaction of contributing in a productive way to collective life and happiness.

For more information visit the center's website at http://petergreenhallchildrenscenter.dal.ca/.

formed its curriculum from traditional to developmentally appropriate practice to one that follows the minds of children—listening alertly to their ideas, desires, and hopes—and supports the children in expanding and developing their theories about the world with strong, purposeful curriculum activities embedded with rich learning" (see "Designing the Environment to Build Connection to Place" on p. 25 and "The Doll Project: Handmade Dolls as a Framework for Emergent Curriculum" on p. 53).

"The fact that I'm interested in their work and that they tell me about it makes it important in a way that it might otherwise not be seen to be: It makes the work more visible to people inside and outside Peter Green Hall Children's Centre," says Carol Anne.

We, the readers, are fortunate this is the case. Because not only are these powerful and insightful stories of professional development that hold rich insights for us, each is an invitation. Whether we spend our days with young children or support those who do, we can reflect on our practice and consider how sharing our stories might give us a new perspective and promote our professional growth.

It All Begins With Relationships

"You look back and say without all of it happening, how could any of it happen. Yet how can you pin down how a relationship grows?" responds Carol Anne when asked how these stories came to be written. "I like the people at Peter Green Hall, I value their work. We became friends. You pay attention to your friends and that's the first step in the writing of these stories."

"We go back," recalls Barb. "We first met in the late 1970s when Carol Anne was one of my professors at university, then met again in the '80s, reconnected, and became friends and colleagues."

"I chose to spend time in this program," says Carol Anne, "because I was touched by how these educators push the practice of child care and education beyond the boundaries of what we have known or thought possible.

"The first edition of *The Hundred Languages of Children* came out in 1993," she continues. "I was excited about it. I took a copy to the center and asked, 'Have you seen this?' They were excited too, and the Reggio experience became a catalyst for growth and change. The Peter Green Hall staff started looking to me for support about what was going on in the field regarding Reggio-inspired practice."

By then staff had started doing documentation. "They were excited about what they were doing," says Carol Anne. "They'd show me, and we'd all get excited."

"Even after Carol Anne moved to Toronto to teach she'd continue to visit when she came home to Halifax," says Barb. "She would come to the center and offer provocations: 'Talk about what you are doing,' she'd say. 'Tell me more. What do you mean by this?' Carol Anne has a way of making you feel that what you say is important. She treats people respectfully, the way we want children to be respected. She listens. She has a sweet, gentle manner. But at the same time she is strong in what she believes in. She doesn't just agree. She brings depth."

And part of that depth is honoring the reality that relationships take time and care. During a sabbatical, Carol Anne spent a day a week in Peter Green Hall classrooms. "Even then," she says, "it took many months to develop enough trust that a teacher would feel comfortable enough to say, 'I mucked up.'"

It's being able to talk about the "I mucked up," "I'm afraid," and "I don't know what to say or do" moments in a teacher's life (in all our lives) that often holds the keys to our most important insights and discoveries about ourselves and others. And positive relationships make those moments possible.

Choosing and Developing a Story

The teachers at Peter Green Hall document their work and that of the children. Using photographs of children at work, samples of their efforts, and text—children's conversations, teachers' thoughts—they keep track of and share with others the intriguing events occurring inside classrooms for young children. At the same time documentation provides an opportunity for those in the classroom to reflect upon their interactions, challenges, and learning. As the staff's documentation helps children be aware of their growth and development, it also makes the stories in this book possible so that the adults at Peter Green Hall—and the rest of us, too—can learn and grow from their development.

"When Carol Anne comes to Halifax each summer she asks, 'What have you been up to?'" says assistant director Bobbi-Lynn Keating with a smile in her voice. "One year, we answered, 'Oh yeah, we did a breast cancer thing' (see "A Mommy Breast and a Daddy Breast: Encountering Illness as Emergent Curriculum" on p. 93).

"'Tell me more about that,' she said. As we started talking to her, she stopped us. 'OK, are you kidding me?' she asked. 'This is amazing work.'"

Carol Anne adds: "We look at documentation when I come back home. I look and listen. I have an intuitive sense that tells me when something is going on that should be lifted up out of practice to become visible to the broader field of early childhood education. I think this is one of my gifts—to see what might be useful to others—and part of my contribution to our work together.

"This is something we should explore," Carol Anne suggests. "If they like the idea of exploring it, we make a plan. We arrange a meeting—one to two hours. I ask questions and take notes. I then take my notes and the teachers' documentation and write a first rough draft. Next, I send it back to each person involved who reads it and offers feedback to me. We talk it through with me making alterations to the draft until we have it written in a way that satisfies everyone."

To choose new pieces to write for this book, Barb and Carol Anne sat down to talk. They knew they were going to write the story of Aaqib. They thought they might write about the center's garden that exists against great odds. But then they considered the Zombie World project and the tensions it created in the center. Female teachers were putting their noses up at it, an interesting tension to explore and attempt to learn more about. Carol Anne says, "I remember saying to Barb: 'Everyone has done a Garden Project. Why don't we do something more of a challenge?'"

Making the Invisible Visible

As Carol Anne listens and writes, she highlights aspects of teachers' practice and introduces ideas so that they can then be seen and become consciously incorporated into teachers' sense of self as professionals and daily interactions with children, families, and each other.

As Bobbi notes: "Because of her tutoring and ability to see, we're getting better at noticing when we are doing something that is different. The greatest gift Carol Anne has given us is the confidence to live and teach in uncertainty. . . to reflect . . . to respond even though you know there is much more for you to learn.

"You think you know it, this practice of emerging curriculum. Then along comes breast cancer, a zombie world, or the illness of a child. And you think 'I really don't know.' Thanks to Carol Anne, I continue to scaffold, building on new knowledge and skills. My colleagues at Peter Green Hall would tell you the same."

In Closing

A firestorm of positive energy for creating, something that Carol Anne calls "the windhorse effect" (Wien 2008, 159), is a major consequence, in her view, of emergent curriculum. This effect occurs "whenever children understand in their bones that their own good ideas will be accepted and supported by their teachers" (this volume, 112).

As Carol Anne says on page 112, "When the children's positive energy is activated, they are flooded with ideas for invention. Love of the work, positive affect arising from their own creating, drives their activity. Adults are invariably astonished at what young children so energized can design and produce, a fact witnessed by the international response to the Reggio Emilia experience (Edwards, Gandini, & Forman 2012)."

> Once children are helped to perceive themselves as authors or inventors, once they are helped to discover the pleasure of inquiry, their motivation and interest explode. (Gandini 2012, 44)

It feels safe to believe that teachers and program leaders, too, experience "the windhorse effect."

As you delve into these stories, Carol Anne asks that you be aware they are not telling you how to do something. "Because practice is so complex and diverse," she explains, "I'm nervous about suggesting that there are right ways that lead to desirable results. Or that there are predictable patterns that others could repeat for the same result. The culture within centers is much more complex than that. In these stories we are merely sharing our experiences for readers to consider."

Carol Anne and her colleagues at Peter Green Hall have "written these stories to see where they are going to go." Now they are sharing their stories in this book. And now it is our turn as readers to see where these stories—and our own—might take us.

....

Amy Laura Dombro, MS, is a writer who believes that stories are a too-often overlooked strategy for change. She works with organizations to document their successes, challenges, and lessons learned so that others can benefit. Amy is an author of *Powerful Interactions: How to Connect With Children to Extend Their Learning.*

Chapter 1

Carol Anne Wien

The Power of Emergent Curriculum

Why did I become so interested in both emergent curriculum (which I see as a North American phenomenon) and in the Reggio Emilia experience of early childhood education? Was it because my own experience of schooling in the 1950s and 1960s was so traditional—workbooks, questions with right or wrong answers, endless sitting and waiting, compliant children? The only escape was daydreaming. There was little opportunity to have a good idea (Duckworth 2006), except in English composition (creative writing), but that too was replaced with critical writing by the time we reached university. I was 25 before I had a strong experience of creative possibility, of finding a voice of my own. In Ithaca, New York, I was assisting in a brand-new Montessori school and enrolled in Montessori training. I was impressed that we were asked to offer respect to children, to observe and listen to them, and amazed by how a "prepared environment" allowed children to initiate activity that absorbed them for long periods of time (Montessori [1912] 1964). In the course I was taking, we were asked to design a new classroom material using Montessori principles such as a built-in self-correction for children. I designed and produced a model tap, a faucet to use with dried beans or peas, mounted on a mahogany wood stand. Twist the solid clear plastic tumbler a quarter turn in its clear plastic surround and watch the beans slip through the hollow pipe inside and spill into the basin below, making a lovely sound. It was a collaborative effort to produce it, and the result was beautiful, functional, and deeply satisfying. To create in this way was a different world than I had known. It was an awakening: What kinds of education permitted such creativity?

Emergent Curriculum and Reggio-Inspired Practice

As a college and university lecturer in early childhood and child study programs during the 1980s, I was grateful for NAEYC's work to describe high-quality practice and to attempt to define it (Bredekamp 1987). Children's ideas, creative designs, and the right to move their bodies struck me as fundamental to their right to learn. In 1989 I happened to visit the exhibit The Hundred Languages of Children, from the municipality of Reggio Emilia, Italy, when it was installed in Newtonville near Boston. Here I saw children's ideas and creative designs expanded and proclaimed in an extraordinary profusion the likes of which I had not imagined possible. A children's project, titled "The City in the Rain," included an astonishing series of drawings of water traveling under the ground. Waist-high dinosaur sculptures were designed entirely using tiny shadow boxes, each box with a child-created installation inside it. "This is really serious," I recall saying to myself, noting that Reggio Emilia required much closer attention from me, for it was clear either their children were extraordinary (a common perception when North American educators first saw Reggio work) or else their educators knew things about children that we did not. Reading the first edition of *The Hundred Languages of Children* (Edwards, Gandini, & Forman 1993) and participating in the 1997 study tour to Reggio Emilia, Italy, were strong markers in my sense of becoming a long-standing student of the Reggio experience.

Reggio-Inspired Interpretations Outside Reggio Emilia

What is the Reggio Emilia experience? The Reggio Emilia experience "is based in the municipal system of 46 centers for children from birth to age 6, owned and operated by the city of Reggio Emilia in northern Italy" (Wien 2008, 2) and sustained by that city for close to 50 years. At first, in reading that 1993 text and attending study tours like so many American educators since the 1990s, I did not recognize their ideas and ways of working as so different from our own: I thought they were simply doing what we were doing, but better. But as Rinaldi spoke on a May day in 1997 about relationality, reciprocity, collaboration, documentation, beauty and delight, the city as context for children's participation, children as producers of culture, and so forth (Wien 1997), I slowly opened to the realization that we might mistakenly think we understood her words in English and easily assimilate them to our own meanings for them, when in fact her Italian meaning might be very different from our North American sense. I became curious about the possible differences in meaning. I wanted to explore them. And, as John Nimmo says, they "exploded my mind" again and again.

I will give an example, as an illustration, to share the way their thinking disrupted my own. What did Rinaldi mean by an image of children as competent and capable? Didn't we have a positive, respectful image of children here? Certainly we wanted to believe we did (Bredekamp & Copple 1997). What did she mean, "To know is first of all to love something" (Rinaldi as cited in Wien 1997, 31)? I was struck by the fact that affect was considered so essential to a concept of knowing. And as Rinaldi talked repeatedly about "relationality," I realized she was speaking of much more than relationships among people, although they were a strong part of the concept. The concept of relationality included relations with materials, places, ideas, and so forth. I surmised that the stance from which children were being observed by adults in Reggio Emilia was different than ours, that they were observing relations, and trying to sustain and deepen them (Rinaldi 2006). I interpret "relations" to mean the connections (or attachments) that children are forming as they engage with the world—relations with people, materials, and places that children orchestrate into an expanding world view. It seemed to me that beginning from a stance of observing and listening to children for the relations they are forming is a different lens than beginning from a notion of observing child development, as is our custom here. They are different, if overlapping, frameworks for practice. To look for child development is to look for what we already know, as in the tendency of early childhood education programs to treat the content of child development as what should be observed. To look for the relations that children are forming is to look for what might be revealed. In the latter, there is a chance for surprise, enlightenment. Who knew, for example, that a child would become so attached to a snail brought into the classroom that two weeks after it was put outside again, he still stands on a chair looking out the window for it (Avery 2013)? He has formed an attachment—a relation—to the snail. To observe relations makes affect, and the directions of attachment of a child, immediately central to decision making: "To know is first of all to love something" takes on some meaning.

But the purpose of this chapter is to set the stage for what you will encounter in the chapters that follow: It is not an introduction to the work of the educators of Reggio Emilia for there is ample material from Reggio itself for that purpose (Edwards, Gandini, & Forman 2012; Rinaldi 2006; Vecchi et al. 2011). Reggio educators have long believed that their education system is not a model that can be copied and transported elsewhere to produce the same results. They think that any program is steeped in its local culture, language, heritage, and history and the results will never be identical (e.g., Spaggiari in Cadwell 2003). Programs cannot be transported wholesale from one culture to another like factory-made goods, nor can they be standardized. Human beings are not standardized and groups of them even less so. The Reggio view is that their philosophy and processes may be *interpreted* by others and in so doing, will bear traces of translation that contain aspects of local culture, both recognized and tacit. The strongest difference between the Reggio Emilia experience and our own, in my view, is the widespread involvement of the city and its politicians in validating the importance of young children, and the education of young children, for the culture and well-being of the city (Delrio 2012; Moss 2012).

Reggio-Inspired Changes in Practice

Although this chapter is not intended as a comprehensive introduction to the Reggio Emilia experience, I highlight here some of the Reggio ideas and processes that have had significant impact on the educators whom you will meet in this book. Our interpretations of these ideas and processes have changed our thinking and practice with children and families, and with students of early childhood education. The reader should note that the practices highlighted here are but a small part of what we know as the Reggio Emilia experience.

The image of children as competent meaning makers. The pivot point of change is to understand children's right to their own experience as the foundation of their lives. Children, as protagonists of their own lives, will make their own meaning from their experience. This complex idea contains the notion of the image of children as competent, resourceful, and full of possibilities alongside the corresponding obligation of adults to support their right to experience their lives. If adults are looking and listening for the meaning that children are making in daily life, their responses to children are very different than if they are trying to teach and control children. The adults' image of our own role shifts from one of needing to manage to needing to support. What does it mean if a child has a right to be a protagonist in his own experience? First, a right to move as the body wants to move and to be minimally confined, a right to be curious, attentive to the world, and to have that attention taken seriously by others, to be able to take action, to have intentions and discover their reasonable limits, and so forth. To be a protagonist is to be an actor in the world. In the chapters that follow, you will see educators grappling with what such an idea might mean in their programs.

Collaboration as a sharing of work, not merely dividing up tasks. A second shift is a change in stance from thinking of work as accomplishing tasks alone to thinking of work as shared in collaboration. Even when we work with another educator in our room we frequently divide up responsibilities, each going a separate way, one monitoring the room as another handles bathroom routines, one settling children as another has lunch. The notion that we could share our experiences with others and discuss them together opens up a different notion of collaboration: It slows us down to consider what is happening in more detail and invites us to ask others to look at what we have noticed, documented, or done. Such collaboration involves sharing experiences and planning and requires administrators to provide time for these. You will see these educators learning to share events together in new ways.

Pedagogical documentation. New processes involved in documenting are perhaps the most radical change in practice undertaken by the educators in this book. Documentation is the generating of observational data through using multiple tools for documenting—such as generating images, videotaping, audiotaping, note taking, collecting samples of children's work—and making it available in some focused forum for others to study and interpret. When we are generating this material we are documenting, a process quite familiar to those steeped in developmental appropriateness. But when the material is studied collaboratively, to gain the ideas and interpretations of multiple participants, it has the potential to become pedagogical, that is, to teach us, because it opens us up to what others see that we did not see and to what we might see that we had not thought to see or to think about. It expands—both widens and deepens—our world of thought and feeling. And it adds a reflective step between observation and teacher response that is very helpful in widening our thinking about possible responses. Out of this expanded perspective we can then imagine responses of higher quality that are more closely crafted to children's experience. We move thus, not from observation of children to linear planning of what to do, but rather from observation and listening to children to thinking together to interpret meaning before planning possible responses. Pedagogical documentation slows us down from our hurried lives to consider a moment of lived life in detail, with attentiveness and appreciation for the meaning of life children are creating. As the Reggio educators say, revisiting documentation makes learning visible (Giudici, Rinaldi, & Krechevsky 2001; Rinaldi 2006).

Multiple modes of representation of experience. Reggio educators refer to "the hundred languages of children" (Edwards, Gandini, & Forman 2012), a metaphor that emphasizes the benefits of experiencing many different ways of expressing our thoughts and feelings, whether it be through painting, music, dance, constructing with blocks or wire, writing, singing, using electronic technology, and so forth. Each mode requires different understandings and actions, as we learn the properties of materials and the techniques for working with them. Each mode can have differing effects on memories that arise and are formed. And different people, of course, become attached to and skilled in different modes, enriching our experience of each other and contributing to the wealth of culture.

Aesthetic sensibilities and design. The term aesthetics is associated with visual art and philosophy of art, but I wonder if it might be useful for early childhood education. I claim it in the sense in which Dewey speaks of it, aesthetic sensibility as a part of daily experience and as a human response to our surroundings (Dewey 1934). To have an aesthetic sensibility is to appreciate and enjoy aspects of our sensory world: It is gray and misty out my window this morning as I write, yet the grass glows an intense green and the tulip magnolia is a creamy, silky pink. Vecchi notes the aesthetic sensibility in children (2010), reminding me of the sculpture project you will meet in a later chapter in which 4-year-olds have definite notions of beauty, and a strong aesthetic response to materials around them. Aesthetic sensibility is also very much an aspect of educators' responses, and we can sense from the tonal quality of environments whether the teachers have thought through design of environments beyond the traditional ordering from a catalog. And the design process, whether it concerns visual ideas for lettering on a panel or the functional tranquility of an environment for children's daily living, is ongoing for teachers. How should this room be arranged to support children's inquiry and engagement? Where should the traffic paths be? Where will the guinea pigs be kept so they feel safe and secure? How can we keep coats and boots from taking up one wall? These are design questions, designs for living together (Curtis & Carter 2003). The Reggio argument has been that function and beauty are not separate, and that beauty and delight are necessary to daily life (Cooper 2012; Rinaldi 2006), and since the city of Reggio Emilia is located in one of the major design regions of the world, it is not surprising that beauty and design are so emphasized.

Engagement with the local community. Reaching outward to families and to the community and drawing them into the life of early childhood programs, becoming central to both, are facets of the Reggio experience that we recognize and struggle with in our North American settings. In order to take responsibility for building relations beyond the walls of classrooms, teachers are required to make a commitment to widening the scope of early childhood involvement in society. We recognize that broadening these connections supports the habit of democratic participation.

In the stories in this book you will see the degree to which the educators have been able to bring these highlighted Reggio values into more conscious connection with their programs. Attending to the hearts, minds, and spirits of children and families could be seen as the core value we are embracing, and such a value means also attending to the hearts, minds, and spirits of educators. Sometimes called inter-subjectivity, which Bruner describes as "mutually understanding what others have in mind" (1996, 117), it is the process of asking of ourselves, "Can I understand what you have in mind? Can I let go of my own mind long enough to grasp what you are thinking and feeling?" This is easy to say, hard to do. And when we do so with the stance of listening for children's competencies, we are so richly rewarded as to become astonished at the power of children's thinking and attachment. But how does our attraction to Reggio-inspired practice and the promise it offers other cultures intersect with emergent curriculum in North America?

Emergent Curriculum

Emergent curriculum has been a pocket of mainstream practice in North America for a long time. Elizabeth Jones was using the term in the 1970s (2012), and by the 1980s we had a sense of it as something beyond spontaneous or improvised responses of teachers and as a consistent support for child-initiated intentions to investigate, to make happen, to create. Educators linked with constructivist approaches have always found a place for the eruption of the creative and thoughtful in children whether through inquiry or the arts (Duckworth 2006; Forman & Hill 1980; Katz & Chard 2000). As I described in an earlier work,

> Elizabeth Jones and John Nimmo's *Emergent Curriculum* (1994) gave a name to a form of curriculum planning that many constructivist early childhood educators had been pursuing for a generation. While Jones had been using the term since 1970, as Carol Copple notes in her foreword to the book, its title gave the public domain a fresh term for a complex, sophisticated teaching practice, a term that brought into relation the notions of an intentional course to follow, a plan with logic, and its apparent opposite, an emergent or unplanned process. The term emergent curriculum thus captures a seeming paradox: an intentional course is implied by the word curriculum, derived from the Latin *currere*, meaning to run a course or make one's way around a known route. But paradoxically, the course of this curriculum is not known at the outset. It is emergent—that is, its trajectory develops as a consequence of the logic of the problem, the particular connections that develop as participants bring their own genuine responses to the topic and collaboratively create the course to follow out of these multiple connections. (Wien 2008, 5–6)

The route emerges as children and teachers together create responses to their own questions. And through documentation, the course can be made visible so that others can see it.

Reciprocal Planning

How should we think of emergent curriculum? Susan Stacey (2009) reminds us that it is first and foremost play: "When children explore through play their own theories about how the world works, they become deeply engaged" (p. 2). Both the schedule and the environment require sufficient open, unhurried time for play to happen. In the early '90s when Susan and I gave a symposium on emergent curriculum, we thought in terms of teacher planning, and of emergent curriculum as an approach to planning that began with observing children's interests. An approach that begins with listening to children, rather than beginning with expectations or standards to be met, asks first what are the children learning, thinking, feeling? What meaning are they constructing from their daily lives? Such curriculum begins where the children are, and turns in their direction first. Such planning implies a suspension in which reflection helps determine responses to children's ideas and interests.

My summary analysis that attempts to describe a "good-enough theory of emergent curriculum" (Wien 2008, see Chapter 11) describes starting points, participatory structures and stances, design work, pedagogical documentation, and a powerful, positive energy that I call the windhorse effect. Has my thinking altered since then? I now believe the foundational element in educators' capacity to create emergent curriculum is the stance of the educator. I believe that educators who construct emergent curriculum are thinking of what they are doing very differently than in mainstream teaching and learning. The best name I can find for this stance, so far, (and I don't find it satisfactory—it needs to be simpler) is aesthetic responsiveness.

Aesthetic Responsiveness

In analyzing the qualities of care found in practitioners of emergent curriculum, I find four qualities—but I'm sure there are more—that integrate qualities of ethical encounters and of creativity. These four qualities are authenticity, attentiveness, appreciation, and empathy (Khattar & Wien 2012).

Authenticity. The term *authenticity* refers to the fact the educator is being himself or herself while professional, that is, such a person is not pretending to be or feel other than he or she is: There is a capacity to reflect on the self, to be honest, authentic. It has to do with a quality of integrity of personhood. Perhaps it is strength of identity, but I find the educators in this book, for example, believe in emergent curriculum profoundly and have an incredible commitment to it. This depth of authenticity comes through to parents and others and assists the bonds of relationships.

Attentiveness. Qualities of listening, of unhurried awareness, of giving over to another are referred to as attentiveness. I think of it as like a suspended breath arcing over a distance like a bridge to reach another: We can feel when others are attentive to us and children recognize a teacher who is profoundly interested in what they are doing or saying. Like meditation it is simple, very easy to say, but much more difficult to do. Our attentiveness is constantly disrupted by unavoidable agendas for action—groceries to pick up, banking, gas for the car—a sort of battle for our attention, which is also our consciousness, a jungle of things competing for our awareness. To hold those back and offer attentiveness to another is a gift to another, a quality of regard that gives the other visibility.

Appreciation. To appreciate is to value positively. It is to hold a positive emotion in mind. Appreciation is what leads me to give the overall term the qualifier "aesthetic." In this stance there is an unconditional positive regard for children, and a disposition to value their intentions. It is the relations the children are forming that strike the adult as beautiful, worthy of appreciation, and may be as simple as a toddler thinking of trying to fit a rolling pin into a Peg-Board: We see he has found another cylindrical shape like the peg, and we can appreciate his idea and his idea of making the game more elaborate to suit his interest (Avery 2013). This capacity to find loveliness in the actions of children is to me profoundly aesthetic and ethical.

Empathy. If we say empathy is a quality of feeling with another, we might also say it is a quality of care, and a quality that leads us toward gentleness with others. Empathy is soothing to both giver and receiver, and creates bonds. Empathy is also reciprocal (Bresler 2008), dynamic, and fluid, and its generation moves back and forth among individuals and groups. It is not pity, for pity is not reciprocal, but rather an integrative feeling that brings people into partnership.

> The term *windhorse* arises from the secular Buddhist tradition called Shambhala (Trungpa 1987). I do not recall where I first came across this wonderful word, but it was sometime after a community of this tradition moved from Boulder, Colorado, to Halifax, Nova Scotia, in the mid-1980s. I apply windhorse here because it speaks of raising positive energy, power like the muscular energy of the horse that carries the rider like the wind yet is able to be directed by discipline and self-regulation, like the rider on the horse's back (Trungpa 1987). There is a powerful positive energy of concentration and engagement and excitement that occurs in classrooms of emergent curriculum: Educators say " . . . it's like electricity" (Thomas 2008) or "You can taste it" (see Chapter 4 in this volume). Since 2008 I have chosen to refer to it as the windhorse effect because that is the closest language I have found to convey this tonal quality of positive, directed group energy based in integrative values (Wien 2008). "Integrative values are concerned with the collective and include conservation, cooperation, quality and partnership" (Tamminen 2013).

Design and Creativity

What does design mean? For graphic designers it means "visual ideas" (Grulovic 2013), but in dictionaries it means something planned or sketched out in mind or plans for something to be created. The word carries both rigorous, narrow meanings and broader, more general meanings. I prefer the wider meanings and use the term "design" to refer to something that children or educators might make. It requires our creativity to design something that does not yet exist for us, and in finding new forms we create new identity and integration for ourselves (Connery, John-Steiner, & Marjanovic-Shane 2010; Csikszentmihalyi 1990).

Rinaldi (2006) believes that creativity is fusional. What does creativity fuse? It fuses intellect (the cognitive) and emotion (affect) and out of this fusion memory becomes durable. Vygotsky thought so too (Connery, John-Steiner, & Marjanovic-Shane 2010). We don't forget something we have designed and made, like my model faucet for the Montessori classroom. I believe design processes, the opportunity to design and make many kinds of things in many "languages of learning"—be they musical instruments, processes for classroom projects, new areas for early childhood environments, new recipes for meals, experiments for mixing colors, sketches for a painting, processes for new structures in institutions—are at the heart of what it means to use our creativity toward what we might invent that is new to us, and perhaps those around us, in the world. To do so brings us more life, makes us excited, engaged, and determined, keeps us curious and noticing things around us, and works against the disconnection and numbness we can feel in the face of overburdened schedules. Emergent curriculum, such as that inspired by Reggio Emilia and by American educators, offers us profound opportunities to develop the creativity, empathy, and participation that sustain us both in daily life and as a society.

Introduction to Parts of the Book

The book is composed of three parts, each with three chapters, and a reflective response from other educators following each of the nine chapters. Part One includes stories of changes in the structure of programs. Part Two offers examples of emergent curriculum with three different age groups of children. Part Three offers stories of difficult life events that became part of daily curriculum. Overall, what we see is a rise in the quality of practice over a 15-year time frame.

Part One: Environments for Living and Learning

The first chapter in Part One, "Untiming the Curriculum: A Case Study of Removing Clocks From the Program," is an important precursor of the changes in practice that occurred among the staff of Peter Green Hall Children's Centre. It was a first, anxious step into uncharted emergent practice to explore what might happen and occurred in the mid-1990s. Susan Stacey was director at the time of a small center operated by a local hospital. When the hospital closed the center, she joined the staff at Peter Green Hall as assistant director. Elizabeth Conrad, one of the toddler teachers in this experience, also joined the staff at Peter Green Hall and has worked there ever since. At the time of writing, I had been speaking about the problems of production-schedule organizations of time for young children for many years, and Susan was the first, to our knowledge, to challenge her staff to break out of that organization of time. We were intrigued by the consequences and, as is my habit, I said something like, "Oh Susan, we should write about this."

The second chapter, "Designing the Environment to Build Connection to Place," highlights work that began in September 2003, when emergent practices were well developed in the program at Peter Green Hall. This chapter shows a sophisticated and thoughtful practice in which the teachers think very carefully about the relations children are forming, including, in this case, relations that resulted from a hurricane that devastated Halifax.

"From Policing to Participation: Overturning the Rules and Creating Amiable Classrooms" comes from a different location, three child care programs in Hamilton, Ontario.

Karyn Callaghan had invited me to talk with a group of program supervisors about changes they were making, inspired by workshops on Reggio-inspired practice that Karyn was offering the community on a monthly basis. She said their process of letting go of rules in their programs had been liberating for educators and held counterintuitive results for children. Their process illustrates well some of the experiences of opening up uses of time, space, and relations that we think are crucial for the development of emergent curriculum. Experiences such as those described here are, we suspect, somewhat typical of educators shifting from managerial practice focused on keeping routines or prioritizing merely health and safety to a rich, experiential practice with deep bonds of relationship forged in many directions.

Part Two: Examples of Emergent Curriculum

While Susan Stacey was at Peter Green Hall she was instrumental in provoking Bobbi-Lynn Keating, Heather Cameron, and Joelle Rowlings to begin an emergent process by having a conversation with 2-year-olds. She also supported the educators throughout this first emergent project by documenting. This project in the chapter "The Doll Project: Handmade Dolls as a Framework for Emergent Curriculum" is a strong marker in our sense of the development of practice at Peter Green Hall because it kick-started processes such as deeper, more attentive conversations, documenting to revisit with children, and consciously slowing down the pace to the children's rhythm.

Valerie Quann and I wrote "The Visible Empathy of Infants and Toddlers" based on her master's research project. In what sense does research into empathy in young children fit discussions of emergent curriculum? While researched as a study of empathy, we also find this chapter shows important aspects of emergent curriculum such as what happens when educators offer attentiveness toward thinking about children's capabilities: We see what we might not previously have seen. To be attentive to such capabilities tends to lead to wider possibilities for action in children, which we think you will see too.

The chapter "Moving Into Uncertainty: Sculpture With 3- to 5-Year-Olds" articulates, to my mind, well-developed practices of emergent curriculum shared collaboratively among staff, children, and an outside friend. Yet it also shows adult uncertainty, wonder, disappointment that some of our processes did not work as hoped, then joy at the way the children surprised us with their interest, self-regulation, and creative energy. Perhaps it shows too our increasing consciousness of trying to show teacher decision making.

Part Three: Difficult Life Events as Curriculum

The three chapters in this final section are emergent curriculum examples from the past five years at Peter Green Hall. "A Mommy Breast and a Daddy Breast: Encountering Illness as Emergent Curriculum" occurred during the 2007–08 year and was written up a year later. How does a master teacher of emergent curriculum respond when she herself is diagnosed with breast cancer? This chapter shows the responsiveness of Bobbi, her colleagues, and the children and families in the center and illustrates the depth of change in constructing relationships that had developed after 12 years of emergent curriculum.

The final two chapters are new work not previously published. "Zombie World: Boys Invent a Culture in Their After-School Program" developed over the 2011–12 year. The difficulty that arose for the educators was the extreme discomfort of the female teachers with the topic and the tension with the two male teachers who supported (and were energized) by the children's engagement. Such a context created a dilemma for us to explore and reflect upon, a reflection by no means completed by the writing of the chapter, but rather opening up the dilemma for discussion with others in the field of early childhood education.

"Aaqib at the Center" occurred during the 2010–11 year. This chapter describes a most difficult life event, the serious illness of a child who is part of the community. Such illness moved outward in ripples affecting, alongside his family, the children and educators in his classroom, then staff and families of the entire center, and to hospital staff. This chapter illustrates Elizabeth Jones' argument that emergent curriculum is what happens (2012), and then illuminates how this life-threatening situation was absorbed into the daily life of the center.

The Arc in the Development of Practice in the Center

An arc is a rising trajectory: It starts in a fixed place and rises in a curving form to some-place else. The overall argument of this book is that the changes in practice enacted by educators over 15 years raised the quality of practice. The arc I see is a trajectory that elevated the quality of practice through four overlapping phases (and of course, traces of all phases remain)—from adult-controlled management to developmentally appropriate to emergent to encompassing difficult life events. When Barbara Bigelow began as director in 1990, practice was traditional adult-controlled management of children, with processes such as tightly timed schedules with frequent transitions, adult-controlled activities, and expectations for children's compliance to adult purposes. Barbara wanted practice that was developmentally appropriate (Copple & Bredekamp 2009). Her first five years saw con-siderable movement in the direction of developmental appropriateness: Staff who wished to support this direction remained and staff who did not left the center. With the introduc-tion to the Reggio Emilia experience and notions of emergent curriculum in the mid-90s, the long struggle to change practice continued to open in new directions and processes, as you will read. In Part Three of the book readers will witness a practice that is able to embrace very difficult life events as curriculum. Instead of hiding or turning away from them, to "protect" children, these events became daily curriculum. The question raised by the content of Part Three is whether emergent curriculum might support a tendency to move in a direction that encompasses life events, that does not turn away from that which is difficult or that which we prefer not to experience. Such events may typically be deemed too difficult for young children, yet you will read how children contributed remarkably in each of these cases.

Watching the rising arc in the development of practice among the staff at Peter Green Hall has inspired and taught me, for their accomplishments take us into areas I had hardly thought possible as curriculum. Educators were able to confront and embrace difficult life events in a way that made all participants accepting of them, and that created a sense of a caring community going beyond what we could conventionally think of as appropriate for children. Such daring is both remarkable and an inspiration. It is a joy to see all this work brought together in one place, so that this arc in the development of practice becomes visible. My hope is that readers will also find pleasure, interest, and possibly inspiration in reading these stories and that the experiences described will help us imagine our capaci-ties to go beyond what we thought was possible in early childhood education.

PART ONE

Environments for Living and Learning

Chapter 2

**Carol Anne Wien
and Susan Stacey**

Untiming the Curriculum: A Case Study of Removing Clocks From the Program

Teacher Elizabeth Conrad glances at her watch and tells the group of toddlers, "Five minutes until tidy-up time." The toddlers (18–30 months of age) are engrossed in play and do not even look up. Five minutes later the staff start to pick up toys, encouraging the children to help and trying to make a game out of cleanup time. The children help to the best of their ability. They are familiar with this approach, for it happens at ten o'clock every day.

M any practitioners in high-quality early childhood settings work with open schedules that follow children's interests and needs, and have done so for much of this century. Unfortunately, in many other classrooms and for many children, unhurried time and sustained attention in activity is being threatened by a "production-schedule" organization of time. That is, if it's ten o'clock, it's snack time—no matter how interested Melissa and Ian are in continuing their block castle, it must be cleaned up and put away until tomorrow. In these early childhood settings, the clock dictates when activities change. The teacher dominates because she is the timekeeper, marking when activities stop and start.

Production schedules, which move items through a series of events in linear, lockstep fashion, emerged with the rise of factories and industrialization in the nineteenth century: They organize time to ensure that specific things get done. Schools for older children adopted the production-schedule organization of time, with separate timed periods for each activity and sharp breaks between them. In contrast, early childhood education has long proposed a holistic model of care and education for young children, with an integrated curriculum, unhurried time, and sustained complex activity (Copple & Bredekamp 2009; Elkind 1990; Hohmann, Weikart, & Epstein 2008; Isaacs [1930] 1968; Jones & Nimmo 1994; Katz & Chard 2000; Montessori [1912] 1964).

Susan Stacey, as a center director, wanted to offer developmentally appropriate practice in her program—a curriculum based on children's needs and interests, support for child choice and child-initiated activity, and unhurried time in which children could sustain activity. Yet even when she hired teachers who supported these values, the classroom routines continued to be run by the clock. Teachers were rushed, trying to implement a certain number of planned activities by a certain time, and at first Susan could not understand exactly what they were rushing toward. At the same time, her teachers would deny it: "But I'm not working by the clock."

The teachers' conscious values supported developmentally appropriate practice, so they did not want to see themselves as following a production schedule. How is it possible that directors and teachers who want to implement developmentally appropriate practice find themselves caught up in time schedules that make this practice more difficult?

All teachers and directors use "scripts" for action performed automatically to get themselves through the day (Wien 1995). Such scripts are patterns of action repeated in the same way day after day until they become taken for granted as normal, expected practice. Teachers have scripts (of varying kinds) for calendar, circle, activity or play time, story reading, snack, bathroom, napping, and so forth. When teachers know these scripts well, they perform them automatically, saving conscious thought for more important events. Since child care programs are organized across the day, teachers quickly adopt scripts for handling time, and these scripts become taken for granted as the obvious or only way of functioning in the setting.

Scripts that use time in a production-schedule way are often inherited from previous teachers and carried on because no one has had time to think consciously about doing things differently (Wien 1996). Because time organization is taken for granted, teachers cannot see how this use of time undercuts the developmentally appropriate practice they cherish. Ambery (1997) noted how children's and adults' time lines clash, and invited comments on handling time in programs for young children. We report here on one 10-month experiment with opening up the possibilities for handling time, and the consequences for one classroom.

This chapter was first published in the September 1998 issue of *Young Children*.

Our Experiment—Eliminating the Production Schedule

When teachers Tanya Clarke and Elizabeth began working together in the toddler room, the morning routine included playtime (about 30 minutes), circle, small group, snack, outdoor time, story, and lunch. The pace was rushed, with the teachers trying to keep things "on time," and there were lots of transitions. Though these teachers were skilled and able to keep the routine smooth, with little waiting time, play (the activity Tanya and Elizabeth agreed was most important) was disappearing due to time constraints.

They had inherited the schedule from the previous teachers working in this classroom and had taken it for granted as the way things were done, even though no one—certainly not the director or previous teachers—had actually told them this. Rather, the toddler teachers had simply absorbed this use of time from living it as they began work in the setting. Since they were new to the center, they deferred to the practice already present. Tanya and Elizabeth were adopting taken-for-granted scripts for organizing time.

At the time, Susan was reading Carol Anne Wien's book *Developmentally Appropriate Practice in "Real Life"* and was struck by the following quote: "Oddly, the only way I know to break this dominance of time organization is to focus attention on the organization of space, to make changes in the environment and watch children's responses, and, in the process, to let time go, let it vary, rather than holding it constant" (Wien 1995, 136). Susan wondered how practice might change if the teachers "let time go." What if formal measurement of time—for example, using clocks—was removed from the classroom? As director, Susan invited Elizabeth and Tanya to remove clocks and watches from their classroom, to keep a journal of the impact of this on themselves and the children, and to focus attention on children's interests and needs in making decisions about program and routine. Here we describe the first 10 months of this process.

A Few Fixed Events, and a Sequence of Events, but Beyond That . . .

The plan was simple: The staff would not wear watches, the room would have no clock. The order of events would remain unchanged, for the children's sense of security. However, the timing of activity changes would be decided according to cues from the children, gathered from teachers' observations. To prepare, the staff reviewed the literature on play rhythms in young children, such as Garvey's "peaks and valleys" (1990) and Montessori's "false fatigue" ([1949] 1969), in order not to end play prematurely because they might misinterpret children's engagement.

The basic frame for the day included some immovable parts—staff needed breaks, nap was necessary, arrival and departure times were set—and this came to be considered the *routine*. Everything that was centered around the children and planned by the staff—such as playtime, circle, small group, outdoor activity—was considered *program*. With the clock gone, staff took lunch breaks "whenever the children settled for nap," and the children ate lunch "whenever they were hungry." Snack was "open" and available during much of playtime.

At First the Teachers Were Frustrated

What happened for Tanya and Elizabeth when they removed clocks and watches from the room? In the first weeks, the formal program disintegrated. They became so focused on what the children were doing that other components of the day simply did not occur. Circle time disappeared, because the children were focused on their play. The teachers did not want to interrupt the children for small group. Outdoor play sometimes did not occur until the afternoon. The staff complained of "feeling adrift" and feeling that "nothing was happening." And one of the teachers was so focused on the children's play that the other felt compelled to complete all routine chores—housekeeping, diapering, hand washing, and so forth. She did not appreciate this change in responsibilities!

The children, however, were very happy. Their play was frequently extended for most of the morning and showed teachers new talents and interests. For example,

> One day, the teachers noticed Mark, a quiet and undemanding child 26 months of age, sorting vehicles. To the teachers' astonishment, he made two groups—vehicles that fly and vehicles that don't. The teachers extended his interest in classification at circle time, inviting children to choose a vehicle and pretend to move as it moves—quickly, slowly, high, low.

As time went on the teachers became increasingly alert to the children's activity and thinking, and the "rushed" feeling in the classroom was gone. However, another tension took its place. The two teachers often disagreed with each other in their interpretations of the children's needs and interests. They discovered they had to renegotiate how to make decisions about when to switch to another activity; previously, the clock had decided for them.

One August day, for instance, they were out walking with the children, a casual walk around the neighborhood with talk about what they could see. The children had lots to say and moved slowly, examining each new item encountered—a squished caterpillar, a familiar cat hiding under a porch. Two children new to the program were not used to walking and quickly became fatigued. One of the teachers thought they should all return to the center. The other countered that the other children were deeply engrossed and had only been out half an hour after a long, rainy week indoors. They were at odds about what to do. Both had the children's interests at heart, but they prioritized needs differently.

For some time the teachers could not agree. Then an idea emerged: One teacher could take the two new children back indoors, and the other could take the other children to the enclosed center playground, where she could safely monitor them. It was the first time it occurred to them they could best serve the divergent needs of the group by splitting up; in this case, one going indoors and one staying out.

In other words, they found themselves imagining and doing quite different things than ever before. Removing the timepiece as the decision maker for when to change activities allowed them to break open the old script for going outside and to imagine new possibilities.

But Then Things Became Better Than Ever

Tanya and Elizabeth's distress concerning how to make joint decisions based on the children's needs and interests led them, after several weeks, to reexamine what they thought toddlers really needed in a program. After what at times were heated discussions, they reached a consensus on an appropriate program structure for this particular group of toddlers: The children needed to be greeted on arrival and helped to make a choice of activity ("planning"). They required a long period of playtime—with snack and toileting taking place naturally within this period but not interrupting it. A short circle time was to remain, because the children so enjoyed the music and action, then some outdoor time would follow. Small-group time would move to after the afternoon nap. This plan reduced the number of transitions significantly, and since there were no watches, no particular times were allotted to the various components.

With the clock removed and play frequently continuing throughout the morning, the teachers experimented with inviting the children to tell them when they were hungry, rather than stopping play and imposing a transition to snack. They offered food initially to one or two hungry children, then one of two things tended to happen. Sometimes, when the first children were finished eating, the teachers would casually comment to those who had not eaten that snack was available. Other times, if the children that day were younger (many of the children were part time, so ages each day tended to vary), a crowd of children would eat at the same time, since they were hungry and found it difficult to wait.

One day several children asked Tanya for something to eat. She brought out oranges, pears, bananas, knives, napkins, and a plate. Four toddlers gathered around her at a small table. Tanya gave each child a plastic knife, and with her support the children began to cut and peel the fruit. This took considerable time—time for sampling, talking, learning to handle the knives, eating as they went. Tanya was unhurried. Snack for these four children lasted 20 minutes, but there was no sense of hurry. Snack would last as long as it lasted. Elizabeth, across the room, supervised hand washing and toileting and brought other children to snack as the first ones finished. In all, snack lasted 45 minutes because the preparation and eating were so relaxed and full of interest to the children. By the time these children went outside to the playground, the older children were coming inside for lunch.

The staff, to their surprise, found that without clocks, this younger age group tended to eat lunch later than the older children in the center did. They also ate very well, wasting less food, and they slept well and without fuss after lunch. When they broke open old scripted patterns and tried out different ways to live events, new discoveries about the children became possible. Who would have thought toddlers would eat lunch late? And why not, if there has been a long and luscious morning snack?

The Script Is a Trap—Opening the Trap

Teachers who value and want to support developmentally appropriate practice are often trapped using scripts that arose long ago out of patterns of teacher management that are still in place in settings today (Wien 1995). A script for teacher management gives the teacher power to control what people do; if the teacher follows a production schedule, the child has little power to alter the time frames set by the clock (Wien 1996). When teachers begin work in a pre-established setting, they must follow the time patterns already in place or they are no help to their colleagues. Nor is it likely that newly hired staff have time to negotiate with their teaching partners in much detail before beginning work. As Tanya said:

> "I was just so happy to be working here. I was new, and everyone had been here longer. I felt I should just follow them, that this was the right way to do things. But it didn't feel right."

But the longer teachers live, day to day, with patterns that don't feel right, the more difficult it becomes to change them.

Once the clock was removed from Tanya's and Elizabeth's work patterns, a new curriculum began to emerge. It did not focus on an arbitrary program that the teachers believed was "good" for the children. Rather, the children now began to co-own the curriculum with the teachers. The teachers' observations were more astute and precise and more cohesively tied to programming. For example,

> Peter spent a long stretch one day playing with small blocks. He was attempting, with great difficulty, to build a bridge. Tanya offered words of encouragement and described his actions back to him: "You're trying three blocks now instead of two. Will it work? What kind of block do you think you'll need now?" After much experimentation and a great deal of time, he accomplished his first bridge.

Before the removal of the clock, Tanya had been too caught up in carrying out the established routine to find the time to watch carefully and support children in such accomplishments, even though she believed she should be providing this support during children's play.

Sometimes the new curriculum that emerged swept through the entire group of children. For several days there was intense interest in babies, for example, and Madeleine decided that she needed to carry her baby in a backpack. The teachers improvised, emptying Madeleine's own backpack of her supplies and popping the doll into it. Madeleine wore the backpack all day, even at naptime, and the following day all of the children were wearing backpacks with doll babies tucked into them. The children insisted the babies accompany them everywhere. When they went on walks outdoors, the teachers provided a stroller from the infant room for the "babies in backpacks" who wished to ride instead of be carried. These extra preparations required time and effort by the staff, as well as obliviousness to embarrassment while walking down the street with a stroller full of dolls in backpacks.

This curriculum about babies was sustained for more than a month, with the backpack phase lasting two weeks. All the children and teachers, for example, brought in their own baby photograph. These were placed at the children's eye level on the wall and were revisited many times, the children seeing new similarities and differences between then and now each time they examined the photos. Gradually the children used the babies at small-group time, dressing them in baby clothes with all their intricate fastenings. This then led to the children dressing themselves and seeing the fastening of their own clothing as an intriguing activity.

Reflections

Production-schedule organizations of time are outdated in an age in which a holistic, integrated curriculum in child care settings is preferred (Copple & Bredekamp 2009; Stacey 2009). However, the desire to implement developmentally appropriate practice does not in itself make it happen. A rigidly kept time schedule undercuts support for children's play, for children's decision making and ownership of their activity, and for children having the opportunity to assume responsibility for their actions. These are all undercut when activity is stopped in order for something else to begin. The message the child receives is that her own activity is less important than the teacher's demand to respond to a change in activity. While there are many occasions in a child's life when adult-imposed change is necessary and entirely appropriate, there are other times when it need not happen. For adults to become aware of the difference between these two conditions requires great sensitivity.

One of the ways directors and administrators can assist teachers in facilitating developmentally appropriate practice is by supporting collaborative reflection-in-action (Curtis & Carter 2007; Edwards, Gandini, & Forman 2012) to construct a more conscious practice. Reflection can allow teachers to recognize taken-for-granted scripts as events to question and reshape toward cherished values. Administrators can assist by providing staff time for reflection; by asking searching questions (not simply "What are you doing?" but "Why are you doing it?"); and by joining discussions in which new patterns are explored, attempted, and evaluated. Susan supported Tanya and Elizabeth by joining them for weekly reflection time to discuss what the children were doing and how they were doing it.

Directors may be interested particularly in several of the discoveries we made throughout this process. Experimenting with time provided a vehicle for taking apart and renewing the program. Everyone learned not to fear the stage when things fall apart; in a sense, this must happen, in order for something else to be invented. Also, if the question begins, "What happens if we do . . . ?" then there is no sense of personal criticism. The question becomes a vehicle to rethink teaching practices in a nonthreatening way. To experiment with time in this way is also a way of engaging the director: Susan became very intrigued by what could and would happen and was as invested in the outcome as were the teachers. Although we describe a case with only two teachers, there was a ripple effect on the center, as other teachers and classrooms became interested in what was going on with the toddlers—how lunch could be eaten so late, why dolls in backpacks were going out on walks.

To remove clocks and watches was a catalyst for change, removing the taken-for-granted and permitting new ideas to emerge.

Time organization is the keystone holding up the arch of everyday events. To remove old patterns of time organization calls into question everything else that teachers do and requires them to reflect on the taken-for-granted scripts for time they inherited from their predecessors. Reflection permits teachers to invent new scripts that may better support their conscious desire to construct developmentally appropriate practice. As Elizabeth said:

> "I don't find it so nerve-wracking now. I thought we were appropriate before, but we weren't anywhere near as flexible as we could have been. [Now] we are more aware of what to look for, what to discuss."

Ten months after removing the clocks, both teachers commented that they felt a new sense of freedom to do what they believed they should have been doing all along.

Elizabeth Jones

Watch the Children Instead of the Clock

When I was a new baby in the 1930s, mothers in North America, including mine, were faced with two competing plans for feeding us: tightly scheduled (every four hours by the clock) or demand (whenever we cried). I don't actually know which plan she followed; the scheduled feeding may have been considered more responsible then, and she was very responsible. But by the time I had my own children, pediatrician Benjamin Spock had become more influential than behavioral psychologist J.B. Watson, and demand feeding was the in thing to do. So, that's what I did.

Cultures differ in the value they place on keeping track of time. This emphasis accompanied industrialization in northern Europe, and Big Ben still chimes over London on the quarter hour. Factories standardized and synchronized tasks in order to produce perfect products. To free workers for the factory, schools took over the education of their children, adopting a factory model by standardizing lessons. Children learned to tell time at an early age and get to school when the bell rang. Independent thinking wasn't generally encouraged (Toffler 1981).

Although much of the world has since become *post-industrial*, with increasing reliance on innovative thinking and new technologies, timing remains a priority in most schooling. It shouldn't. A high-tech international society needs initiative, creative thinking, and respect for diversity—individual and cultural and environmental. When everything changes so fast and information is available to everybody all the time, standardized solutions don't always work. You have to be practiced in creative thinking and interested in the unexpected to survive and be an intelligent contributor to democracy. True, it's complicated; democracy has been described as "the worst form of government—except for all those others that have been tried" (Churchill 1947). Democracy is messier day to day, and much more complicated, than authoritarian societies where everybody knows their place. But democracy is necessary, for the world's future.

Letting Go of Teaching by the Clock

Time remains a priority in most schools and child care centers. As the authors of this chapter explain, "All teachers and directors use 'scripts' for action . . . to get themselves through the day. . . . When teachers know these scripts well, they perform them automatically, saving conscious thought for more important events (p. 14)".

Compared with elementary schools, care and education for under-fives has offered greater flexibility, focused on development more than on standardized teaching. That was easier to do when the preschool years weren't seen as significant. Now that they are, even by politicians, schooling models creep downward. When teachers are required to bring all the children together for a long daily group time in order to cover the material in a curriculum guide, the clock must be watched. And the flexibility of play-based learning has been lost. Schools, as many of us know from our own childhood experience, are traditionally bound by clock watching. In many educational settings supervisors expect teachers to be skilled production managers, able to control children's classroom behavior and efficiently follow a standard curriculum. As preschools have become more like primary schools, teachers of young children may find themselves expected to assume responsibility for enforcing the rules and following the daily schedule, without variation.

It All Begins With Little Children

"No point in starting anything there. They never let you finish," said my son about his second grade classroom. If you let the children finish what they've chosen to do, what will happen? Problems, no doubt—and opportunities to *think*.

In this chapter two toddler teachers find themselves in the middle of a dilemma. They are recent hires at a preschool that voices a developmental philosophy, yet has historically followed a prescriptive time schedule. Consequently the teachers believe their role is to herd eight 18- to 30-month-olds into a semblance of group behavior. The teachers don't have to negotiate with each other about what to do when: It's group time, bring them inside. The program director, who has been frustrated by this structure, offers teachers a challenge. What would happen, she asks, if we remove all clocks from the classroom? Your task will be to "let time go"—to watch the children, and yourselves, instead of the clock.

Democracy for toddlers? Well, perhaps not all the time—but how can they learn genuine respect for others if they don't experience it for themselves and if they don't have continual opportunity to practice decision making?

> Democracy (like play) is about
> . . . making choices
> . . . negotiating choices
> . . . sharing decision making
>
> With these skills, continually honed for the rest of one's life, one can thrive as a responsible member of a democratic community. (Jones & Cooper 2006, 31)

Choosing, negotiating, and sharing are all time consuming. Clocks get in the way. After untiming the curriculum, how can teachers be responsive to the genuine differences among the children, seeing them as strengths rather than as problems?

Transforming Problems Into Provocations

As the authors reveal, untiming the curriculum becomes a gift for the children, and their interests create remarkable emergent curriculum for the whole group. But this process took external control, that is, a scripted curriculum, away from the teachers. The teachers had to learn how to problem solve with each other when facing real choices. Nobody can get mad at the clock; it's just a machine, and it's always right. Clocks depersonalize conflict. At first readers may wonder if the removal is a gift for the teachers or a whole new burden.

Working by a clock is a march, carefully timed. It requires obedience rather than thought. Working without a clock is a dance, with room for collective improvisation. It requires continual attention to the movements of others, and to the potential for beauty.

Inevitably, teaching is to some extent a dance, especially when it involves teaming with a partner. If that partner treads on your toes, thus resisting your ideas or proposing ideas you don't agree with, you have a problem—a personal problem.

Can a problem be a gift? Is collaborative problem solving a part of getting along with colleagues so you can all support the children in your care?

In a preschool with no clocks, teachers have lost their traditional convenient guides to what's supposed to happen next. Instead they have to pay attention to the children—and to each other. That's more work. It's also more interesting. It asks them to decide what to do and to build friendly relationships in order to collaborate. Those challenges are remarkably like our learning goals for young children. Teachers, like children, need to play with possibilities in order to get smart. Clocks, like canned curriculum, regularly interrupt play opportunities. Teachers at play recognize themselves as "teacher-researchers," investigators of what's happening.

Self-initiated teacher research transforms teaching problems into *provocations*—adult play with a purpose. *What's going wrong here? How can I figure it out? How can WE figure it out? If we try this, maybe that will happen. Let's try it tomorrow, and take notes, and talk about it.* This is probably the best way to become a better teacher; certainly the books written by teacher researchers are some of the most readable and memorable stories out there. And stories are what we remember best.

....

Elizabeth (Betty) Jones, PhD, is faculty emerita in human development at Pacific Oaks College in Pasadena, California, and coauthor of the NAEYC books *Emergent Curriculum* and *The Lively Kindergarten: Emergent Curriculum in Action*.

I am grateful to my colleagues who have written this reflection and the others that follow each chapter for their interest and for their voices, which form a sort of choral support for the work that is described in each chapter. My partnership with a few of those writing reflections is new, and I especially appreciate the willingness of Mary Benson McMullen, Travis Wright, and Marian Marion to step into the landscape created and offer responses. Others are colleagues whose friendship and thinking I have valued for many years, and I thank Laurie Kocher and Veronica Pacini-Ketchabow, Margie Carter and Deb Curtis for our ongoing exchanges. Still others were important when I first entered the field as a fledgling author: Elizabeth Jones and Carol Copple offered support as I was stepping into an academic role, and their response to my work encouraged me to continue. Lella Gandini, with her warmth and graciousness, brings hope to many for the work we might do, and Carolyn Pope Edwards offers gifts of intellectual acuity and integrity. And to have our beloved Canadian colleague Sue Fraser within these pages is a blessing.

—Carol Anne Wien

Chapter 3

**Carol Anne Wien,
Annette Comeau,
Bobbi-Lynn Keating,
and Barbara Bigelow**

Designing the Environment to Build Connection to Place

How do teachers respond, first to a crisis in their center and then to a larger crisis in their city? And how do these crises affect their design of a child care environment for 3- to 5-year-olds? This chapter shows how an environment at Peter Green Hall Children's Centre shifts, evolves, flourishes, and builds connections among children, staff, and place as teachers respond to local crises.

Aspects of the Reggio Emilia experience with particular resonance for Peter Green Hall include these concepts: children as rich protagonists in their own experiences, with knowledge and creativity to contribute; teachers and children as collaborative partners in long-term learning; learning made visible through documentation; and the impact of visual aesthetics on the functioning of the environment. We have long recognized that a beautiful, caring, sensitively organized environment makes a major contribution to the sense of belonging, comfort, safety, and capacity to be responsible and productive of all participants in the setting (Cadwell 2003; Curtis & Carter 2003; Edwards, Gandini, & Forman 2012; Kritchevsky & Prescott 1977; Shanker 2013).

The Center Addresses a Crisis and a Challenge

In September 2003 the center faced a crisis. All three staff members in the senior room (for children 3½ to 5 years of age) were leaving (one for a job opportunity, two on maternity leave), and no suitable candidates had applied for the positions. Barbara Bigelow, the director, wanted to move either Annette Comeau or Bobbi-Lynn Keating from the junior room to bring stability to the senior room. But Bobbi and Annette worked well as a team and were unhappy at the prospect of giving that up. After an intense day of discussion, the agreed-upon solution was that both Annette and Bobbi would move to the senior program. Appropriate accommodations were made for the junior room.

The challenge for Annette and Bobbi in their new classroom took two forms, the physical space and the state of the children. The room is a big box, some 20 by 30 feet square, with hard surfaces and harsh fluorescent lighting. By far the biggest issue was noise levels. Bobbi thought it the "worst-acoustic room" she had ever been in; Annette thought she would go crazy; and Carol Anne Wien, when she visited, felt like her ears were full of shards of glass. Child care center classrooms are often so noisy as to cause auditory fatigue in children, much higher than the 30–75 decibels optimum for recognition and processing of speech (Munro in Willis 2000). The senior room also has little natural light due to the eastern exposure of all its windows.

When Bobbi started working in the room, her initial approach was "to ride the waves," absorbing the room's disordered functioning. Annette's approach was to explore; she opened a cupboard, and things fell out. Their first discussion acknowledged their sense that the senior room children "did not have respect for themselves, the teachers, or the materials." Something about the climate in the room suggested that much positive energy had drained from it. We hypothesized that the poor acoustics and harsh fluorescent lighting affected the children's behavior, leaving them debilitated and drained of energy.

How should they begin? Bobbi says, "We knew from our previous environment that the children needed a connection with the room; we knew they needed to be part of what it was going to be."

First Actions

This chapter was first published in the May 2005 issue of *Young Children*.

There may be as many ways of facing challenges as there are styles of teaching. Bobbi and Annette's first response was to strip the environment, to aid their own understanding of the classroom dynamic, and to clarify the schedule to bring a more predictable order to the children's day.

Stripping the Environment

"We have to be able to work" was the teachers' feeling. Over the weekend, Annette conducted a giant sort and clean of everything in the room, throwing away broken items. Next, the two teachers removed furniture that reduced sight lines and created sound and aesthetic problems. A storage shelf that was too high was cut down to child height. The teachers began a new organization for materials stored in cupboards, acquiring recycled plastic bins for small materials and putting a photograph of the contents on the front of each bin. The room was cleaned and painted.

Part of the stripping involved removing damaged doors from two plywood cupboards. In one, the doors were replaced with a curtain, to help soften sound. In the other, the teachers discovered a beautiful set of narrow floor-to-ceiling shelves. The shelves were perfect for the display of many interesting items in transparent jars, which the children could explore and use in making things. Bobbi and Annette believed that once the environment was clean and organized, they would be able to see their next steps.

Clarifying the Schedule

"We had an appreciation for some exciting aspects of the program," Bobbi says, which included a long, uninterrupted play time. The senior room schedule, however, had been loose, with lunch occurring spontaneously as children expressed hunger. Bobbi and Annette felt that this lunch hour flexibility left the children anxious and occasionally aimless, and that it contributed to the disorder. Annette says, "We sat down and thought about how every minute of the day should be in terms of the children's comfort, and how efficiently it should work."

One of their first responses was to create a stable, predictable schedule for themselves and the children. They kept the long play times in both morning and afternoon, but fixed lunch at noon and nap from one o'clock to two. "We knew we wanted a good family-style lunch—a social event. So we now have tables where each child and teacher has a place: It's like a dinner party."

For the transition from lunch to teeth brushing to nap, each child has a small activity tray. The children and teacher who arrive earliest in the morning choose beautiful materials to put on the trays for each child to explore after lunch. Each day the trays are different and a surprise. They might contain a mix of materials, such as several small rings, colorful ribbons, and some small animals.

Another response was for the teachers to keep consistent work shifts: The same teacher would always be there early in the morning, and the same one late in the day. This decision required some sacrifices on their parts, as only one teacher would ever go home early; but they believed it necessary to bring stability to the program. It was not long before the children responded positively to the consistency in the schedule.

A Big Vision for the Environment

Influenced by the Reggio philosophy, Bobbi and Annette knew it was important to include natural elements in the classroom, but did not yet know what direction enacting this value might take. They also wanted the environment to reflect a sense of the geography and culture of the city so that the children could experience a reflection of those aspects while inside. .

During the stripping, cleaning, repainting, and reorganizing of the classroom's time and space, the teachers and children went on outings. One field trip took them to Halifax's famed Point Pleasant Park, 85 acres of forest on a peninsula jutting into the ocean harbor. Later the teachers noted the children's avid interest in the things they had seen in the park—mushrooms, red squirrels, birds, trees with many leaves. They thought the children's interest in the forest might provide the vision around which to develop their environment.

They discussed their ideas at length. Annette went through magazines, cutting out pictures that fit their vision, then sketched a two-page spread that showed images of forests, colors of golden stone and gray boulders, sun and shadow, various greens, and a pergola made from tree trunks and branches. Based on their observations of the children, Annette and Bobbi knew the major areas they wanted to create in the classroom, and they mapped them onto their design for an interior forest. Their idea map indicated trees, a water feature and a riverbed, a glade, a sandy beach, a bridge, and an organization of space allowing organic rather than purely geometric shapes. The pictures and the idea map show the vision, the dream for what they could make, of this environment. These events took place in early to mid-September.

A Crisis in Halifax

The night of September 28–29, 2003, Halifax was struck by Hurricane Juan, a Category 2 storm that caused Category 3 damage. The last hurricane to hit Halifax had occurred in 1893— before our time! We had no idea a storm could wreak such destruction. Trees were toppled into streets, and power in the city was out for days, in some areas even weeks.

The hurricane had slammed into Point Pleasant Park, snapping and toppling 75 percent of the trees. The park was closed (not to reopen until the following June). When the children went on an outing to a different park, they crawled among the toppled tree roots. The teachers found the children very concerned about the trees: "They wanted to take water to save the trees," and they poured water on the roots and patted them with bits of sawdust "so they would come alive again."

The children, of course, were not the only ones in shock; so was the entire population of Halifax. How do teachers respond in such conditions?

Annette and Bobbi responded by finding "trees" to take into the classroom. Several were limbs from trees in Bobbi's yard, and several were from the neighborhood, reclaimed from the curbs where they had been set out for garbage collection. Soon there were seven trees in the classroom, seven-foot-high branches, stripped of their leaves and cemented into green plastic pots. The trees softened the interior space, adding a filigree of organic forms in the upper spaces.

Annette said, "The children were very concerned about the toppled trees, so creating a forest in the classroom was the right direction to take." Using fallen branches as trees for the classroom acknowledged and made visible the children's concern. It also served as a small act of purposeful construction in the face of the grief everyone in the city felt over the loss of so many beloved old trees.

Changes to the Classroom

Even with the trees added to the classroom, the harsh elements of noise and lighting required attention. Annette and Bobbi continued their reinvention of the classroom environment.

Improving Light and Sound Levels

Annette's experiences in theater led her to believe that color transparencies used to filter spotlights (called "gels") might soften the quality of light in the classroom. She spoke to a lighting expert (sound and light technicians at rock concerts or local theaters are good sources of expertise), and together they experimented with orange and green filters over the center's fluorescent tubes to create a more incandescent effect.

In researching solutions to the sound problem, the teachers found that the high-tech solutions available would cost the center $3,000. This was too costly. But in the process, Annette and Bobbi gained insight into what was needed and found technical experts willing to offer advice.

Two walls of the room are faced with gray melamine below a thin chair rail. The melamine, while easy to clean, contributed to high noise levels. To counteract this, the teachers covered the walls above the rail with four-foot-high horizontal panels covered in a warm beige fabric. They filled the spaces between windows with smaller panels, and covered the windows with valences of the same fabric. The beige panels act as sound absorbers.

The two teachers constructed the panels themselves, covering half-inch fiberboard with eggshell foam and topping it with fabric. They purchased the fabric at a local fabric store, with the pleading for financial mercy usual for public child care centers with no funds for capital expenses. Volunteers installed the panels.

Two noteworthy points about the panels are their cost and efficiency. The total cost was $250, plus 18 hours volunteer labor. Most significantly, sound no longer ricochets off the walls and voices can be heard with ease.

Display and Documentation

Carol Anne commented to Annette and Bobbi that the room used to be full of documentation (panels that include samples of children's thinking and feeling in many media) on its upper walls. The walls now hold the bare acoustic panels. Bobbi said the bare walls represented their conscious choice to restore order and calmness. Annette said, "The empty space helps make it tranquil," that the walls would stay bare to allow the eye a place to rest. Bobbi said their use might change at some point, in response to the dynamic of the room. Then they smiled at each other, comfortably tolerating the tension of this difference in opinion.

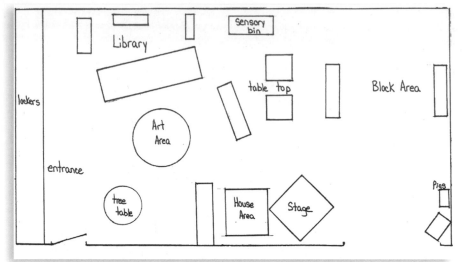

The documentation in the room is now displayed at lower heights, sometimes on the back of a materials shelf, sometimes in three-dimensional form on top of a shelf or in the entryway. The entryway includes a communication center—a cut-down music stand that holds the senior classroom program book. The program book documents each day's activities with a page of description and a page of digital photographs taken during the day. When parents arrive, they look at it with their children.

The top shelf of the wide art shelves at child height contains an interesting display of work by the children. On mini-easels are paintings of cats. In front of these are small Plasticine figures of lions and cats constructed by the children. Beside these is a photograph of Nova Scotia folk artist Maud Lewis and one of her paintings of a cat. The interest in cats arose when one child was looking after kittens for the SPCA. The display makes clear that things that are carefully made matter, and that grown-ups as well as children make such things.

A map of the room shows eight areas. The entryway extends along the short wall of the room, with one wall covered with cubbies. From here the children enter either the library near the windows or the art area. Further into the room, on the window side, is a sand/water/tabletop area and opposite it, housekeeping and dramatic play. In the far corner on the window side is an open, carpeted area for blocks and meetings. Across from it is a pathway to the bathroom, with the large guinea pig cage against the wall. While Bobbi and Annette had plans for the guinea pigs to be elsewhere in the room, this is the spot Tuft and Smoothie prefer—at eye level with the children and with a wall at their backs.

The Studio Area

The studio area, a rhomboid shape, is at the heart of the classroom. It is the first area that children enter after saying goodbye to parents. The area is framed by two sets of shelves, with two worktables inside. One of the tables is small and low, with a teacher-made "tree" (see p. 29) seeming to grow through the middle. The tree table is the children's favorite place to work. It evolved from a table that was about to be discarded. Annette and Bobbi cut the table in half, positioned it around the tree, and nailed it back together to try out the idea of having a table under a tree: "We wanted to see if the children appreciated the idea, if it was worth it. It turned out to be the most popular table." The teachers hypothesize about why that is. Perhaps it is the stools or its lowness to the ground, or perhaps the sense of enclosure and quiet breathing space created by the feeling of being under a tree.

The Power of Emergent Curriculum

The Forest Pergolas

The most compelling forms in the classroom are two large pergola-like square constructions. At first glance they look a bit like canopies one might find on rustic four-poster beds. Four small branching "tree" trunks (about four inches in diameter) define the corners in each space. The branching treetops are joined by a framework of large twigs. One structure has an open top and frames the housekeeping area. The other has a loose, organic lattice-effect top of branched twigs. It frames the stage area. Each space creates a sense of enclosure, with a clearly defined inside and outside. Yet they are transparent and easy for the adults to monitor. Both pergolas offer possibilities for multiple uses suggested both by children's interests and by the teachers' delight in furthering those interests through their own ideas.

Housekeeping. The housekeeping area includes a tiny hutch with beautiful dishes, a table and chairs, a tiny stove with a white enamel kettle, and an array of household utensils hung against a coding scheme on a Peg-Board. A wicker baby carriage and a doll sit nearby, and hooks on the posts hold occasional accessories such as purses. The area is free of clutter even as the children interact inside it.

The stage area. This area is an empty space left free for claiming by children's imaginations. The stage area has a bare floor. A portable stage or a small carpet can be placed in the area. Children or teachers hang scarves, masks, hats, and dress-up possibilities from nodules on the pergola's trunks. Wicker baskets offer props. They may tie large fabric pieces between branches to act as walls or backdrops. They can drape a gauzy soft green curtain over the front of the pergola to create a stage facing the carpeted area, so an audience can participate.

The two structures were made over a three-day weekend in an astonishing burst of creativity. Inspired by the pergola in Annette's design sketch, Annette and Bobbi built them in a pioneer-like process. Driving a truck into the Nova Scotia woods (with permission), they sought trees of the right size that had been felled by the hurricane. They hand-sawed them to transportable dimensions, piled the trees on the truck, and brought them to the center. That was the first day of the weekend. On the second day they built the two pergolas. On

the third day they maneuvered them into place. As the teachers moved them, the stage structure happened to be turned at an angle, in a diamond shape, next to the housekeeping structure. It seemed more interesting at an angle, sculpting several spaces around it, and the shape has withstood the test of the children's use and interest.

Ongoing Design and Assessment of the Environment

Which areas of the room are the teachers most pleased with in terms of how they function, and which do not yet function as they might wish? They are delighted by the children's response to the stage area and to housekeeping, and they are intrigued by the children's love of the tree table. In general, the studio area functions well. Once an area works well, Bobbi and Annette tweak it to get it "to do more." An example in the studio area is a new system of palettes and jars for choosing paint. The children enjoy it. The teachers like the library with its adult-size park bench, rack of books, and fish tank for observation, but it isn't "soft enough." Nor does the bench function as they expected: No one sits there. They notice and think about this.

The tabletop/sand/water area awaits its transformation by bringing the forest indoors, according to the design. Annette's vision includes a sandy shore next to the window and a dry riverbed leading into the window side of the block area.

The block area has accessible materials, a large building area on a carpet, and ample and carefully ordered storage. It is safe and clean, and it looks like block areas in other programs. Yet the teachers say it is the least defined area at the moment. Annette feels it is not aesthetically pleasing.

Does it matter whether an activity area has more than a utilitarian design? Annette argues, "If things are presented in a beautiful way to the children, then they have more respect for them. They interact with them in a different way." The teachers plan to cut a 12-foot-square forest green carpet into a curving, organic shape. Plans are emerging for the dry riverbed of small stones, the water feature, the bridge, and the cave.

How do the teachers know when the design is right? How can they tell when an area, and the room as a whole, works superbly? This question presumes that teachers, who operate with tacit expertise implicitly guiding their decisions, can make explicit to outsiders all the multiple strands, ideas, and reasons (both rational and intuitive) that make up the discerning judgment that is the mark of any professional practice (Polanyi [1966] 2009; Schön 1983; Wien 1995). Bobbi says she knows if an area works well based, first, on how children use it—"if there are no experiences of conflict that break down" into disrespect for self, others, or materials. Second, if the area allows children to create and to act purposefully, with concentration and enthusiasm, if it helps their ideas flourish into expression, the design works. These essential criteria have been fulfilled, in the two teachers' judgment, in the housekeeping area, the stage area, and the studio area.

For these teachers, the block area has not yet been designed; that is, it has not yet been brought into connection with their forest vision for the room. It has not been made into a bigger gift from the teachers to the children—acknowledging to the children their care for the trees that were lost in the hurricane.

Reflections

Carol Anne sees an important tension in the design of both space and time in the classroom. Uses of time and space, and possibilities for curriculum in this room, all coalesce into a matrix of experiences that hold children safe during their day—safe to investigate, collaborate, generate ideas, make things and friends, and fall in love with the world and its possibilities.

Time

Outside several fixed points in the schedule, the children and teachers participate together in creating the structure of their days. They make spontaneous decisions, such as including in an outing to the library a visit to a nearby store. The children know their ideas are taken into account in the decision-making process. Paradoxically, the design of time is both highly stable and predictable for basic needs, and highly participatory and malleable—even spontaneous—during activity times. It is an example of the "both/and" thinking that successfully replaces the "either/or" thinking of earlier developmentally appropriate practice (Bredekamp & Copple 1997; Copple & Bredekamp 2009).

Space

A similar tension operates for the design of space. In some ways, the design is fixed and stable. Areas are defined by their function. Materials are stored in specific places and always returned there. The teachers control the quantity of material so that while much is available, there is no sense of clutter. In some areas, like housekeeping, there is a one-to-one matching map of items and their storage. Many items are stored in baskets, which are a lightweight, natural material, yet easy to clean. Other items are stored in glass jars on narrow, beautiful shelving: The shelves look like they hold jewels, and they pique

the children's interest. Simultaneously, within areas, there is tremendous room for and expectation of children's creative exploration of their own ideas and much material with multiple possibilities for use. Every area is for making things, and all areas suggest the use of imagination, whether playing Mommy and Baby in housekeeping or fishing in the stage area, building a city in the block area, making lions and cats in the studio area, or reading in the library.

Goals

What is the ultimate goal in the center? Barb says hers is to give teachers the power to do everything necessary to create strong relationships among children, families, the community, and the center. In this center, teachers have a high degree of freedom to decide what to do in their classrooms. Barb gives the teachers the same freedom that she wants teachers to give to children and families. One result is staff stability—many have stayed more than 10 years. Bobbi's goal is "to create a place where children learn they have good ideas—and they can make those ideas real." Carol Anne sees this as the cultivation of the imagination. It includes all the child's capacities for thinking, feeling, and valuing.

The teachers' design of space and time provides "multiple languages," to borrow a term from the educators of Reggio Emilia (Edwards, Gandini, & Forman 2012), with which these thoughts, feelings, and values might find representation and expression. This cultivation is held within the larger vision of bringing the forest into the children's lives in the center. It illuminates how teachers model "the having of wonderful ideas" (Duckworth 2006) and create structures that reflect those ideas. Cultivation of the imagination is spurred by the actively engaged imaginations of two teachers who find in each other a complementary collaboration that takes design of environments to new heights of originality and connection to children's love of place.

> ## Questions to Ask About Your Environment
>
> - What range of activities do children need to experience in this space/time, and what is the range of choices and possibilities available?
> - To reduce children's stress, how can teachers offer the fewest transitions and the most uninterrupted time?
> - Different areas of a classroom have different powers of stimulation. How do children use each area? Where do they go? What areas do not entice them?
> - Where do negative behaviors occur, and how does the environment contribute to these responses in the children? How can teachers change the environment to promote positive interaction? What would make each area more beautiful and inviting?
> - What energy do you feel in the environment? What contributes to that energy?
> - How are local culture and the geographical location of the center reflected in the environment?
> - In what ways do you see the children, families, and teachers present in the environment?
> - What do you see if you change your perspective, viewing the room from floor level, child height, a ladder? What's apparent that you don't see from adult height?
> - What connections to the environment do the children make? How can they be enriched, along with enriching relationships and attachment to place?

Margie Carter and
Deb Curtis

Observing the Work of Intentional Teachers

Hearing details of the process a teaching team goes through to redesign a less than desirable classroom can give us a fresh way of thinking about the early education environments in which we work. As you reflect on this chapter do you think the protagonists are the children or the adults? Clearly the authors of this chapter are guided by strong beliefs that go beyond conventional thinking about room arrangements or decorating. Central to their thinking is that children need to be involved in what the room is like. This is a very different approach than having a standardized view of a quality environment, with typical designated learning centers, a specified number of multicultural items, and a schedule that requires particular amounts of time be dedicated to addressing mandated learning objectives. The following is a dialog prompted by our reflections on seeing such thoughtful educators at work.

A Child-Centered Environment

Margie Carter (MC): I'm intrigued by the tension between the adult's and the child's role in making an early childhood environment child centered. The initial classroom environment Annette Comeau and Bobbi-Lynn Keating inherited provides few opportunities for children to be empowered to take charge of their learning. Empowering children is an important value for these educators, and they demonstrate for us how educators can think deeply about environments, not just meet standards or high scores on rating scales. By their own testimony the teachers experience the room as hard, harsh, and noisy with little positive energy and "disordered functioning." So many early childhood educators work in environments like this, often without even recognizing the sources of both their and the children's stress. They choose, as Bobbi initially does, to just ride the waves. Clearly they, along with the children, feel disempowered.

Deb Curtis (DC): Similarly, I think sometimes educators may believe their environments are child centered when in fact the children are surrounded with bright, overstimulating colors and commercial plastic materials someone assumes that children like. They may be willing to live with the disorganization and clutter that result from children's lively play because they believe this reflects a place for children. Fortunately Annette and Bobbi have a deeper understanding. They know that order and organization create a sense of calm that allows children to focus and engage more deeply in their pursuits. This is a true example of being child centered since the educators understand that the source of the children's strengths and abilities come from inside the children rather than from the external, attention-grabbing environment that can distract and agitate everyone.

The Value of Acoustics and Aesthetics

MC: I so appreciated that the adults recognize the role that both acoustics and aesthetics play in helping children enjoy their time and focus their play and learning. They are wise enough to turn to experts outside the early childhood education field for strategies to soften the quality of light in the classroom. This is an example of being resourceful and connected to others in the community. I often think that the work of theatre people and music sound technicians could teach us a lot because they too are focused on creating environments for play and focused attention. Rather than living with problems that we don't know how to address, I think it's important for teachers to get better at engaging others to help them find solutions.

DC: I too appreciate that the teachers recognize the importance of acoustics and aesthetics. I have come to more fully understand the importance of careful attention to aesthetics in environments as I have studied recent research about brain development in young children. Children have very flexible brains and they actually hear, see, and experience more than adults do. Children's heightened sensory awareness allows them to notice more beauty in the world along with becoming easily overstimulated in environments that are harsh and loud. It's no wonder the children's behavior changes as a result of the careful improvements that Annette and Bobbi make.

I am impressed with how the teachers work with a small budget and find solutions to enhance the environment. They are resourceful in turning to others for help, and they have their own intuitive sense about how to create a beautiful, peaceful place for children. How can we be inspired by Bobbi and Annette to enhance our eye for organization, visual literacy, and design in our environments? In my own work with children's environments I have also turned outside the early childhood field. I look for interesting materials and design elements at garage sales and thrift stores. I observe the children closely to see what they notice and are drawn to. I also continually try to educate myself on the elements of aesthetics and design by studying interior designs and natural landscapes that convey a sense of calm and beauty, wonder, magic, and whimsy. I ask myself what are the details in this space that promote these elements. How are colors, textures, light, and shadow used? How are the space and materials arranged to create a sense of order and focus? I bring these same questions to my environments with children. What are the elements and organization of the spaces that the children are most drawn to and stay focused in? Annette and Bobbi have inspired me to include in my thinking the notion of a "sense of place" that children can resonate with from the community around them.

MC: The "sense of place" is an important factor. Annette and Bobbi remind us to consider not only giving children a sense of connection to nature in their environment, but also fostering a sense of their particular place and geography. Their sensitivity to the children's attachment to trees is matched by their awareness of the environmental crisis in their community. We are living in a time of climate change and many places across the country are experiencing dramatic weather events as did the children's community in this chapter.

DC: It does seem increasingly important to engage children in deepening connections to the natural world around them. Annette and Bobbi understand and respond to the innate curiosity and concern children have for nature and living things. Including the tree branches and other elements from the natural environment in their room is a unique and beautiful way to cement the children's bonds to their distinctive community. They also provide a way for the children to feel more secure by taking on responsibility of caring for these special trees in the face of the crisis.

MC: Teasing apart the ideas that guided the positive changes Annette and Bobbi begin to make, I see they understand the concept of the environment to include both the physical space and social and emotional climate created by their schedule and routines. They describe thinking about every minute of the day in terms of the children's comfort and how to make it work efficiently. How often is the children's comfort at the center of planning our schedules? Keeping long, uninterrupted play times for the children and creating interesting routines with materials for transitions demonstrates how teachers can keep children's perspectives in mind while figuring out how to work efficiently.

DC: Yes, we can see underneath the educators' thinking and their understanding of the tension between open time for children's easy flow and choice and the importance of predictability in the routine. Both of these elements are critical for children to develop the ability to initiate their own activities and focus and sustain their attention over time. When educators direct children's time throughout the day, children learn to look outside of themselves for what they should be doing. They have difficulty regulating their own actions. But when there is no predictability as Annette and Bobbi describe, children don't learn to take responsibility for being contributing members of a group that can function well together. Annette and Bobbi understand that careful consideration of time is a critical element of a calm and focused environment and contributes to the child-centered philosophy they believe in.

MC: Overall, this chapter reminds us that teachers can work together on innovative approaches to designing children's environments, despite different perspectives they bring to the process.

DC: I am inspired by Annette and Bobbi's dedication to making these huge changes to their environment despite barriers of budget, resources, and differing perspectives. Other educators can learn from how these two teachers valued the particular dispositions and skills they brought to this work. They obviously have strong understandings and a belief in the deep importance of the environment for children's play and learning. They are unwilling to live with what they inherited because they knew the huge difference it would make in their time together. They also have a passionate connection to their community and a desire to heal after the crisis. Because of this they are willing to put in extra hours to get the work done. They are persistent and find ways to enlist other people's help to figure out how to complete the tasks.

MC: And behind the scenes they have concrete support from their director, Barbara Bigelow, who takes the calculated risk of asking them to move together to tackle a problematic room. Directors play such a crucial role in unleashing this kind of initiative among their staff. Kudos to Carol Anne Wien for offering "thinking support" during these huge changes and through her writing, which puts the spotlight on their thinking process from which we can all learn.

....

Margie Carter, MA, is the coauthor of eight books and, as a member of Harvest Resources Associates, works as an early childhood consultant. She is a widely sought after speaker and regularly leads study tours to New Zealand to learn from their inspiring early childhood system.

Deb Curtis, MA, is a teacher of adults and children and has coauthored several books with Margie Carter for early childhood educators, including *Designs for Living and Learning: Transforming Early Childhood Environments*.

Chapter 4

**Carol Anne Wien and
Karyn Callaghan**

From Policing to Participation: Overturning the Rules and Creating Amiable Classrooms

"We were playing outside after a rainy day, and there was a huge mud puddle the size of a large table, and of course a rule about no playing in the mud—children get dirty. The children played around the perimeter of the puddle, digging with shovels and throwing rocks in and watching them splash. Then some started tapping their toes in the water. We thought, well, that's okay, they're wearing boots. Then they were up to their ankles in water. We were really hesitant but thought, what's the big deal? It's only mud. But then we were anxious: They are going to be really dirty, what will the parents say? Before we knew it, they were jumping off the bench into the mud puddle, tumbling over each other. They were covered in mud. We were all standing back, kind of white-knuckling it and thinking, should we let them? We decided yes, and went to get the camera."

How did the staff of three child care centers transform their work lives from continuous policing and correction of young children to a pedagogy in which they and the children participate together in constructing richly lived events? How were they able to let children engage in such wild activities as playing in a fresh mud puddle? The experience we describe here shows that, contrary to common sense, aggression, accidents, and stress from constantly enforcing classroom rules are all reduced and transformed when many of those rules are eliminated by staff in a collaborative process.

The process of reexamining and then removing multiple rules for children's behavior permitted fuller participation in the life of the centers and led to an overall transformation of power relationships: Both teachers and children gained more power to affect what happened in the programs. While reexamining the rules was not the only thoughtful process undertaken by the teachers, it seemed to be especially powerful in opening up practice toward more expansive living. Simultaneously, teachers reexamined the physical environment (organization of time and space) and the ways it contributed to a stressful atmosphere that generated aggression. As Karyn Callaghan, leader of the workshops to reexamine practice, comments, "The whole question of letting go of power just flies in the face of [established] practice."

Established Practice in the Centers

The three nonprofit centers—McMaster Children's Centre, Templemead School, and Scott Park Children's Centre—serve children ages 3 months to 10 years in Hamilton, Ontario. The three settings are on a university campus, at a workplace, and in a high school, respectively. All three centers are inclusive settings, with resource-teacher consultants for children with special needs. Staff are qualified early childhood educators, and the centers accept early childhood education students in practicum placements. As an example of diversity, in one center 40 percent of the families served use English as a second language in their homes, with 10 percent being newly arrived immigrants. Cultures and languages of the families include Mandarin and its dialects, as well as Spanish and Portuguese. The centers serve many single-parent families and families with two parents on shift work.

In all three centers, the established, conventional practice was rule based. Yet staff believed they had few rules and no problems as a result of the rules they did have. Children's safety was the highest priority, with rule setting often justified as necessary to prevent harm to children. However, in creating the rules, the educators did not consider the possibility that harm might come to the children—and the teachers—in other ways as a consequence of these rules. As Karyn notes, "Safety; you can justify any rule with safety."

Another of their justifications was government requirements—that is, the authority of the official regulating body. Sometimes these regulations were real; sometimes they were assumed to exist by the teachers, but in fact did not. Teachers' anxiety over being responsible for young children's lives was clear. Rules proliferated out of fear for the safety of the young and vulnerable charges.

Supervisor Bobbie-Jo Gramigna described how her center had been "very structured." For example, "we had pictures of three faces" defining how many children were permitted in a location, and "children were not allowed to take toys [from one play area to another]." Director and teacher Brenda Gardiner, at another center, said, "You always had to go down

This chapter was first published in the January 2004 issue of *Young Children.*

The Power of Emergent Curriculum

the slide feet first, and you always had to sit up going down the slide." Laurie Jeandron, then a supervisor, notes that in her center, which serves many children with special needs, staff were "stopping things from happening all day long." For instance, a rule said only four children were allowed in the water play area, so any additional children who tried to join the play were redirected to another activity. In all three programs, the time segments for activities were brief, play spaces rigorously defined, and play areas small and tight. In one center, for example, its two separate playrooms each had precisely the same interest areas, all of them small. With tightly defined spaces for every activity, teachers felt they were acting like traffic cops, directing children to available spots.

To give an idea of the tone at the centers during their rule-governed regimes, here is a partial list of what children could and could not do. One center discovered they had 26 rules for outdoor play, including this sampling:

No swinging from the slide.

No crashing riding toys.

Only run in one direction.

No sitting on balls.

No using big brooms.

No banging on shed.

No licking the door.

Staff at another center found that they had many indoor rules, including such specifics as the order for eating food at lunch, as well as these:

No blowing on food.

No other toys used with playdough.

No toys traveling around the room from area to area.

Sit in the same seat for lunch every day.

When Carol Anne Wien asked the educators to define a "rule" in such practice, teacher Melita Veinotte said, "Something necessary to keep control." And *control* is conceived as? Several supervisors responded, "Children obeying" . . . "Children doing as they are told." Brenda added, "It was a comfort for teachers to know there was a rule in place and everything would run smoothly." "Ah," replied Carol Anne, "you believed that this control would in fact work! . . . [a chorus of yeses] . . . But in fact it didn't, because you were policing all the time!"

The effort teachers spent on enforcing the rules to govern the children was immense and highly stressful. Laurie said, "The energy the staff were expending on policing the center, redirecting children, and giving time-out was just so draining." She described the block area at her center,

"Children would go in, and things would start flying, blocks would get knocked over, kids would get pushed, and there would be yelling and screaming. Half the time you would not want the block center open because you couldn't deal with it. It was so loud. That whole half of the room would get really crazy. The noise level would go up and then children would start bouncing off each other and teachers would start pulling out their hair. You could make a comedy movie of it."

Reexamining the Rules

How did changes to practice begin? Karyn offered workshops for the early childhood community in the Hamilton area in which the match between values and practices was examined. Influenced by interpretations of the Reggio Emilia experience (Cadwell 1997; Edwards, Gandini, & Forman 2012; Hendrick 1997; Vecchi et al. 2011), she invited teachers to explore their images of children, and she gently questioned some scenarios observed in the community; for example,

Teachers told children what position to lie in on their cots.

No toys allowed from home.

Weekly themes planned for the entire year without considering children's changing interests.

Staff from all three centers attended. In the workshops, Karyn proposed they think about children's capabilities, and asked,

"If we believe each child is unique and to be respected, and yet we are making children finish all the food on their plates before they get to have a drink, or there are designated times when they can go to the washroom, then what must our view of them really be?"

This notion of a teacher-regulated child forced to follow prescribed institutional scripts for living had not occurred to those attending the workshop.

The invitation to consider the contrast between the rule-based scenarios seen in their centers and the lovely images of children to which the teachers gave lip service prompted Bobbie-Jo to challenge teachers at her center to rethink their rules. This process was difficult. When they tried to discuss the rules as a group, individual teachers reacted so strongly to others' rules, laughing and making faces, that they all had to make a rule not to be judgmental about rules! The teachers described so many rules that the group could not deal with all of them in one session.

The group decided to have a second meeting, with a focus on one area only—outdoor play. This strategy worked, and allowed the staff to note its 26 teacher-generated rules for children's play. This was many more than they thought they had, but their rules had never all been written down before. Bobbie-Jo noted, "Individually, we each had only a few rules, but when you put all those rules together, for a young child there were a lot of different rules, because staff all had different expectations."

Collaboratively, the teachers decided on three criteria for a rule: Did the behavior targeted by the rule harm the child? Did it harm others? Did it damage property? With these criteria in mind, the group began to examine their rules. Someone noticed that play areas were closed when parents picked up children. Did this rule meet the criteria? No. So, the teachers asked themselves, why do we have those areas closed?

Applying the new criteria to their existing rules opened up the process of discarding rules. On the outdoor playground, for example, the 26 rules were reduced to 5:

1. Riding toys are for riding.

2. Riding toys stay off the climber.

3. Sand in the sandbox.

4. Safe bike riding.

5. Hockey sticks stay down.

Here's an example offered by Bobbie-Jo to demonstrate the self-questioning process that could lead to rule reduction.

One day a child brought in a new action figure and told Bobbie-Jo about it. A teacher interrupted:

Teacher: "That needs to go in his cubby."

Bobbie-Jo: "Wait a minute. Why?"

Teacher: "Because it's not his show-and-tell day."

Bobbie-Jo: "Let's put this in an adult perspective. Suppose on the weekend you got engaged. You come in with your engagement ring and want to show everybody, and I say to you, 'Whoa, whoa, it's not your day. But you can put that in your locker.' It's the same thing."

Teacher: "Okay, he can keep it in here [the classroom], as long as he shares it with everybody."

Bobbie-Jo: "I can go along with that, as long as I can have a turn wearing your jewelry when you're done."

Bobbie-Jo argues that while there are many toys to share in centers, "not everything is for sharing."

"If it's not okay for me to borrow another adult's jewelry, watch, or sweater, I don't think it's okay for us to *expect* children to share their things."

Teachers worried that welcoming play materials from home would not work, and they called Bobbie-Jo to come and see how upset children were the first few times such toys were brought into class. Gradually, it became easier to permit items from home to be part of classroom life. Melita said, after eliminating rules about bringing things from home, "It really reduced stress. You are not in power struggles with children." Brenda added that "parents really appreciated it, too," not having to struggle over telling a child to leave a precious item behind. Children's self-investment in their belongings shows an attachment to their identity, and separating from something that contributes to that identity is emotionally difficult.

Bobbie-Jo was the first of the workshop participants to provoke a reexamination of rules and rule making in her center. She gave a presentation on the experience at a local teacher network meeting two months after the initial workshop. After handing out copies of her center's revised list of reduced rules, Bobbie-Jo says, "The audience thought it was completely crazy. They said, 'I would like to see you come and do that at our center!'" Improving classroom safety and harmony by removing rules seemed counterintuitive.

At Laurie's center,

"We started to abandon the rules, and then understood their impact on both children and teachers. We were dealing with 'behavior' on a regular basis. We asked ourselves, 'Why are we doing this? Why are only four children allowed in water play? How is that promoting children's development?'"

The teachers at Laurie's center began opening the water play area to as many children as wished to play there and found that the focus for the teachers became one of negotiating and developing children's social skills for entering play. The teachers made the water table more accessible, pulling it away from the wall so children could crowd all around it. The playdough table, too, went from having three places to many places. Instead of maintaining order, the pedagogical goal became "giving children the skills to learn to enter the situation," such as problem solving how to make another place to play when an area was "full."

Overall, the teachers in all three centers found that eliminating rules reduced stress. Karyn was struck by their process of negotiating rules when incidents arose, with teachers asking one another, "What do you think about this?" Children were invited to join the discussions when teachers asked, "Do we need a rule about this?"

Of interest is the fact that the changes and their consequences were consistent across the three centers and that the changes appeared quickly, over months, not years.

Changes in the Physical Environments

Reducing the rules in their setting, and experiencing positive change as a result, also led staff to explore the organization of the physical environment. In Laurie's center, the aforementioned block area was reorganized and enlarged (from 24 square feet to 200), with much better results for the children. Teachers also found ways to permit block structures to remain standing during cleanup, so children could return later and continue building. This meant redesigning the layout for cots at naptime, but teachers did it, now that their priority was children's activity rather than adult convenience. The impact of the change astonished the teachers. Laurie noted,

> "The mania in the block area just started to die down. Children began to interact in a much nicer way. There was less fighting because there was more room. Children were not bumping into each other. There were more materials available. There were fewer rules about what you could and couldn't do, and therefore the teachers, instead of having to stand over the children and police them, could go in and participate. They could build with the children. They could draw, take photographs, go get other materials. There was a lot more spontaneous interaction."

Surprisingly, it was also much quieter. In addition, teachers in this center found the incidence of accidents and aggression decreasing. A government requirement calls for all centers to complete accident reports for any injuries. One year, among 12 children there were 42 injury incidents—33 accidental and 9 due to aggression (hitting, spitting, biting, tripping, and so forth). The next year, after the center had reduced its rules, incidents were reduced considerably among the same 12 children—of 25 incidents, 21 were accidental and only 4 due to aggression. While many factors affect accident rates, the teachers' perception was that the reduction resulted from the changes in pedagogy. This both was remarkable to them and corroborated their sense that the changes they made resulted in much more positive environments for children. The entire emotional tone of their center is more positive.

Other changes the teachers made included softening the physical environment, such as creating conversation areas, adding Monet prints and flowers to bathrooms, and inviting parents to contribute family photos. Brenda says, "I love the fact that each of the three centers is different."

Consequences of Changes in Pedagogy for the Children

The biggest effect of reducing the number of rules was that settings became quieter and calmer, with less fuss about enforcing minor rules. With fewer rules, less monitoring to do, and calmer children, staff could participate more fully, engaging with children in their activities. The teachers developed greater interest in following the children's lead, such as permitting them to interact fully and vigorously with a mud puddle in springtime.

Brenda made a videotape showing children deeply engaged in block play, woodworking, playing with LEGOs, and dramatic play in the classroom loft. Half an hour into the video, children are still playing in the same areas. Laurie comments, "When children made their own choices, the time spent at activities increased." Children's concentration spans for self-initiated activity became long and sustained.

The children began to generate their own rules for themselves and for others and to involve themselves in self-governing, a process necessary to the development of willpower (Shanker 2013; Vygotsky 1976; [1930–1935] 1978). For example, at Bobbie-Jo's center a group of boys made a space for hockey on the small playground, with rules about how to swing the hockey stick ("Not off the ground"). They made a net and demarcated their area with pylons. Such opportunities to generate rules for group activities make people feel they belong to the social group. Feelings of belonging are essential to any notion of community, and to the commitment of members to that community.

From Rule-Driven, Clock-Driven Practice to Values-Based, Responsive Pedagogy

The teachers felt several things happened simultaneously. The examination of rules, the teachers' surprise at the number of rules, and the subsequent reduction created new degrees of freedom for both children and teachers to act spontaneously. As they let go and gave more control to the children, the children learned that the adults thought of them as capable. This process of reducing rules stood out as momentous in its impact on changing practice. And staff began to see new possibilities for practice. Several teachers joked about their previous focus on time and efficiency: "I remember always looking at the clock, thinking, *Okay, let's go, let's go*; how many kids can you get to pee in five minutes?"

Previously, children were lucky if they had 15 or 20 minutes in an area. It was often 20 minutes of play, 5 minutes of tidying up, 5 minutes of transition, and then play in a new area. A teacher noted, "Time was a rule." Time was a rule that could not be broken. Time as a production schedule, and teachers as keepers of the schedule (Wien 1995), produced policing to maintain the schedule. With the changes in stance, practice was more relaxed, less clock driven.

Karyn saw teachers taking more ownership of their practice. They wondered to themselves, "What do I like?" and "What's driving me crazy?" and saw possibilities for changing

to practices that they preferred, chose, and assessed for themselves. Carol Anne argues the teachers were removing themselves from the established scripts for institutional routine and inventing new practice to fit their own contexts.

All the teachers found that the changes reduced stress. The energy of policing, correcting, and giving time-out was exhausting for teachers; it created negative energy, tearing at the emotional well-being of staff and children. Laurie says, "That energy is now turned into facilitating social interaction among children, exploring their interests, and actually talking to children." With staff chatting with and observing children more, the children are receiving more positive attention and, according to the teachers, "there are fewer behavior problems to deal with."

The teachers have noticed increased calm among the children and a sense of emotional satisfaction. For example, after the vigorous mud-puddle play, the wet and dirty children had to be cleaned up, and their clothes washed and dried before parents arrived. Melita said,

"It was the calmest, most easygoing change and cleanup ever. I couldn't believe it. They sat and helped each other. It was amazing, and we noticed that, as we were right in the middle of it."

Resistance to Change

All the teachers noted the role of resistance in the process of change. Laurie says, "When I entered practice in 1984 or '85, I was very much a controlling sort of teacher. I was very consistent, [thinking] this is the fastest, most convenient way we could get it all done." She adds that after the radical change in her practice, it was interesting to look back on the way she had been. The teachers agreed that it is difficult to think there are better ways to function as early childhood educators. The old scripts for rules generated stress, but teachers thought the stress was due to children's *behavior*. Carol Anne thinks it requires a positive image of children in order to see the routine scripts themselves as a source of stress.

Bobbie-Jo recalls that when she began as supervisor, one teacher said, "You're that Reggio girl, and don't think for a minute you are going to do that here!" Whatever interpretations people make of the term *Reggio*, advocates of the Reggio experience note that at first, they create their practice out of whatever provocations stimulate a sense of ownership and participation in their own teaching. "Of course we're not going to force you to do anything," Bobbie-Jo says she responded to the teacher, and proceeded to talk with staff about their views of children and what they wished to see in the center. She described how later, after practice had changed, a staff person who had been especially resistant was overheard telling visiting teachers the results of following the children's lead: "I can't believe what a difference this has made. I am no longer stressed when I go home!"

Teachers Take Ownership of Their Practice

What happened and how did it happen? From the teacher educator's perspective, Karyn believes a crucial moment in changing practice—the routines for taking action in a setting—was beginning with teachers' images of children and childhood. To start with the view of the child is pivotal. Making a positive image of children explicit permits a conscious investigation of whether teachers' current pedagogy supports or contradicts a positive image of children. When teachers see mismatches between their newly explicit image of what children can do and their teaching practice, that's when they begin to see openings for doing something different that better honors their values.

Once the reexamination of established practice had begun, possibilities for teachers' participation in creating their own pedagogy opened up. Teachers asked, "What's possible?" or "Do you think we could . . . ?" Bobbie-Jo notes that at this early stage "the adults are doing exactly what we will end up doing with the children. In Reggio [-inspired processes] we are asking the children, 'What are the possibilities on this? . . . What can happen? . . . Make your theories. Let's try it out. . . . Let's revisit that.'"

What happens is a change in teacher stance. There is a new disposition to think in terms of possibilities, to invent in response to context—an aspect of good constructivist teaching (Forman 2002). Laurie commented that this change requires redefining what it means to be a good teacher, and that expectations for job performance also have to change. Teachers are no longer "*keepers of the routine*" (Wien 1995), programming according to the production schedule, but *partners* with children. If teachers take control of their own practice, and of assessing the match between their values and their pedagogy, then teaching becomes not performing a job to someone else's criteria but, instead, living in responsiveness to children and families and sharing a broad sense of possibilities about all the ways to participate together. Something about the change is profoundly democratic, if democracy is conceived as full creative participation of all members of the community.

About the Artists at the Centre Project

McMaster Children's Centre, Templemead School, and Scott Park Children's Centre are all involved in the Artists at the Centre Project. Originated and coordinated by Karyn Callaghan, the project brings professional artists to work with children, teachers, and families in Hamilton area centers that explore the Reggio Emilia experience.

This research was supported by the Hamilton Community Foundation. For more information on the Artists at the Centre project, visit www.artistsatthecentre.ca.

Conclusion

The emotional tone of the three centers has changed from surveillance, in order to enforce the rules and schedule, to one of positive, even joyful participation. There is a release of energy, a "raising of windhorse" (to borrow Carol Anne's favorite phrase of the Shambhala Buddhists)—a new, positive energy. Karyn says, "You can taste it when you walk into a center. You just feel there is this life there." Bobbie-Jo adds, "You can feel it, the energy rising: It is just so exciting."

Vecchi (2002, 56) reminds us of Gregory Bateson's phrase "the pulsing of life," as one element relates to another and both change in response. Part of what makes rising energy so exciting is that the changes are occurring collaboratively for the group. Karyn describes the changes as occurring

> ". . . within the context of a real community of learners. We were coming together regularly and sharing these stories, bringing in documentation, bringing these lists of rules, and there was a fabulous sharing in the community."

There are now three more centers in their second year of reorganizing their practice, and six others have joined the process of reexamining their rules. In her former practice, Brenda says she "couldn't wait to get out at the end of the day," whereas "working this new way is like being on vacation."

We thank Bobbie-Jo Gramigna, Laurie Jeandron, Melita Veinotte, and Brenda Gardiner, the child care supervisors and teachers who were interviewed for this chapter.

Marian Marion

Reflecting on Rules and Making Room for Messy Play

The opening vignette in this chapter is worthy of filming: Teachers nervously watch children gradually work their way from digging at the edge of a mud puddle to splashing right in it. The teachers know the center's rules prohibiting such joyous, albeit messy, play but wisely decide to ignore the rules in this case. Startled at the outcome of the hearty play episode, teachers describe calm children who later willingly cooperate with cleanup.

Like these teachers we all have struggled with the occasional clash between our cherished beliefs about how children develop and learn and our practices. In my heart, I, as a young teacher, knew that children derived unbridled joy from sensory experiences. I had seen it firsthand as a student—children's finger, foot, or spatter painting adventures, playing in mud, painting with big paintbrushes and water, water and sand play. As a teacher, however, I also quickly understood the realities of teaching in a school where different ideas about children's learning prevailed. Administrators often do not understand active, play-based learning, and some parents fear the potential messiness of some activities. The teachers in this article seem to recognize this dilemma, and I think that their initial hesitation reflected the culture's aversion to messy play in a school.

It took great courage for them to take that first step toward messy play, and the teachers themselves use the mud play episode as the beginning point for serious self-reflection about classroom rules and control in general. They focus on their stated views of children and about how the excessive number of rules was out of sync with these views. The teachers take the first step in a journey of examining their rules. They list all the existing rules, come up with criteria for absolutely essential ones, and then reduce the number. This reflection is not always a smooth path for the teachers but is done with goodwill and respect for colleagues.

It is important to note that the teachers do not just discard all the rules but instead carefully examine each one. They decide that there are too many rules and reduce the total number to those that are indeed meant to protect the children's health and physical or psychological safety. The net effect of reducing the sheer number of rules benefits everybody, children and teachers alike.

Children Benefited From Teacher Reflection

Children benefited greatly from their teachers' reflection on reducing the number of rules in the classroom. One old rule involves limiting work time in learning centers, with children required to stop playing, clean up, and move on to another center even if they did not want to leave. When teachers change that rule, children can work longer in the centers they select, and this increased time benefits their learning and development. Some learning centers, such as the water table and block area, are redesigned to accommodate more children for play. After rethinking the rule about tidying up every center after every play period, teachers allow children's work, such as block structures, to be left standing for children to return to and complete in the future. This move alone enhances a child's memory, planning, and creativity.

When teachers focus on essential limits but do not go overboard with rules, children tend to develop positive and healthy self-esteem. They feel worthy and grow in competence and a healthy sense of control. The teachers involved in rethinking the number of rules send the message that the children deserve the teachers' reflection, that they are worthy of their teachers' time. Children's sense of control, including self-control, increases when they are encouraged to make more choices for themselves. Again, it is not a free-for-all but a safe environment where children's choices are possible and respected.

Along with the reduction in the number of rules, the classrooms' physical environments change gradually as well, which benefits the children. Carol Anne Wien describes some of the physical changes as a "softening," which shows up as conversation areas, art prints, family photos, and flowers. A softer physical environment contributes to a reduction in children's stress. Along with the increased space and time for play, the changes to the physical environments create a more pleasant and relaxing space for children. Teachers observe that there is far less aggression after implementation of the changes to the physical environment and a reduction the number of rules.

Teachers Benefited From Their Own Reflection

The teachers also benefit when the number of classroom rules is reduced. Monitoring and supervision is an essential and necessary part of a teacher's responsibilities. However, the teachers in these classrooms realize that the large number of nonessential rules had resulted in the need to constantly police the children's behavior. They find themselves spending too much time reprimanding children for infractions of the rules. This results in a great stress for the teachers. So, reducing the number of rules leaves teachers far calmer at the end of each day.

Another wonderful outcome of reducing rules is that teachers have more time for observing and assessing children's development. One teacher, for example, films children engaged in dramatic play, block play, and working with LEGOs and is astounded to see the deep and extended play episode.

The teachers also work with colleagues in tackling the issue of the excessive number of rules. They talk things through. They deal with disagreements. Through it all, they work as professionals, doing the hard work of reflection and subsequent changes. Their work, as they are delighted to see, creates peaceful and productive classrooms for children in their care.

....

Marian Marion, PhD, has been a professor of early childhood education and child development both in Wisconsin and at Governors State University. She is the author of a child guidance textbook in its ninth edition.

PART TWO

Examples of Emergent Curriculum

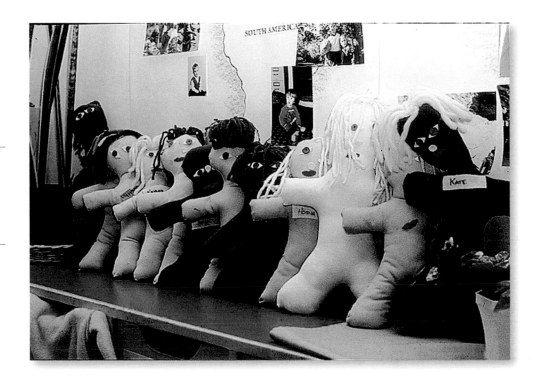

Chapter 5

**Carol Anne Wien,
Susan Stacey, Bobbi-
Lynn Keating, Joelle
Deyarmond Rowlings,
and Heather Cameron**

The Doll Project: Handmade Dolls as a Framework for Emergent Curriculum

What happens when teachers give a 2- or 3-year-old a handmade cloth doll with no facial features? Heather Cameron, Joelle Deyarmond Rowlings, and Bobbi-Lynn Keating were the teachers in the juniors room (for children 27 months to just over 3½ years) at Peter Green Hall Children's Centre. When they began a project on body awareness, they thought it might last a week. Instead, the experience lasted from January until the end of June, when half of the group of 21 children moved on to another classroom. The children's interest, involvement, and development astounded teachers, parents, and supporters of the project.

How the Curriculum Emerged

This emergent curriculum began with a simple idea. The teachers noticed that the children were charmed by babies and frequently took out classroom dolls for washing, feeding, combing, carrying about, and putting to sleep. This play recurred over a period of weeks. After consultation and collaboration with others, the teachers decided to offer each child a handmade cloth doll without distinguishing features.

Gandini (1998) describes a *provocation* as something "arriving by surprise." How would these very young children respond to the provocation of a simple doll to choose, to hold, to attend to, and to think about? We all wondered what would happen.

A network of relationships developed behind the scenes. Art consultant Rhonda Wakely-Fortin designed and constructed the dolls in a resplendent variety of skin tones and body shapes, from skinny mahogany to plump peach. She also devised simple felt shapes for facial features and hairpieces, which she enclosed in plastic zipper bags. Barbara Bigelow, the center director, and Susan Stacey, the assistant director at the time, contacted Carol Anne Wien, who passed on ideas, books, and articles about the Reggio Emilia program in Italy and about emergent curriculum.

Always interested in innovative practice, Barb invited the staff to read portions of *The Hundred Languages of Children: The Reggio Emilia Approach to Early Childhood Education* (Edwards, Gandini, & Forman 1993) and to think about project work based on the children's interests. Susan, who sat in on early planning meetings with the teachers, challenged their thinking, disseminated key readings, and prodded them to begin the project. She also provided practical support for documentation (such as videotaping, taking photographs, getting photos developed); worked with the teachers to turn their documentation into finished panels for others to view; and transcribed conversations to be included with photographs and drawings in the teachers' portfolios on individual children. But the project itself belonged to the teachers and the children.

The pedagogy of project work was new to the teachers. Susan, excited by Hendrick's (1997) descriptions of work with the ideas of Reggio Emilia, suggested starting the project with children's conversations. To the teachers this seemed an unusual way to begin. But ideas from outside our own culture often seem strange at first. Then, as we work with them, they become interpreted through the lens of our cultural understandings; they are transformed as we process them within our range of experience.

Thus, it was with some trepidation that each teacher showed a small group of children a sample cloth doll and audiotaped their conversations. (Where we include children's comments, they are selected from audiotaped conversations as examples of the language responses of the 2- and 3-year-olds.) Presented with one of Rhonda's hairless, faceless creations, the children's comments varied:

> "It's a baby. I have a baby."
>
> "It has no eyes."
>
> "I have a baby in my belly."
>
> "Me too."
>
> "It has no eyes, no lips, no teeth, no mouth, no hair either."

Next, the teachers offered a basket with many different dolls. Each child chose one and the teacher glued on a name label. What would happen next? Nobody knew.

The Primacy of Eyes

The children, without exception, focused initially on the lack of eyes on the dolls. "My doll cannot see you," said David. Interesting! The teachers invited the children to study their own eyes using mirrors. One boy pulled down his eyelid, saying, "Red eye. Look, Bobbi,

This chapter was first published in the January 2002 issue of *Young Children*.

red." Another said, "My eyes are brown in there"; and someone else pointed out, "My eyes are white. Bobbi, see the white? There's black, too. Let me see yours, Bobbi."

Together the teachers and children made a simple sorting chart, on which each child placed two circles representing the color of his or her two eyes. With mirrors close by, the children reexamined their dolls, discussing with the teachers what color the eyes on the dolls should be. Then, using felt pieces of different colors from the plastic bags, the children attached eyes to their dolls with fabric glue.

Joelle admits that she struggled hard "trying not to control" where children put the eyes on the dolls. The teachers used mirrors and talked about the eye placement in a factual way, but did not challenge the children—"We just described back to them what they were doing." Three girls held their dolls up to the mirror, making them look at each other and talk. Aline said,

> "My doll has one blue eye and one green eye. She likes them like that."

The teachers made sure drawing paper and pencils were handy, and some children began drawing faces. (See Julia's first drawing of a face.)

Julia's first drawing of a face. "It's a face, round."

To further investigate and think about eyes, the teachers planned a visit to an optometrist's office. The children took along their dolls on the bus, holding them up to the windows and showing them things. They were very excited as they walked through the mall; many dolls developed weak necks because the children showed them things so vigorously.

At the optometrist's the children tried on glasses and sunglasses and talked about seeing. The teachers took photographs and gave the children drawing materials to record their reactions. Heather put glasses on two dolls, and the children looked at the dolls in amazement. Their comments:

> "My mommy, my daddy—glasses."
>
> "Beautiful!"
>
> "They are holding from your ears, Joelle."
>
> "My doll sees a lot of things."

After the visit, the teachers expected that the children might want to make glasses for their dolls. But Joelle reports,

> "Not one child said their doll needed glasses. We had to let it go. They enjoyed trying them on and putting them on the dolls, but that was enough."

Overall the teachers were astonished at the amount of time the children were absorbed in examining and thinking and talking about eyes—not days, but weeks. When would their interest shift, and to what? Then the teachers heard children's comments change: "My doll has no hair" . . . "My doll's head is cold." Such comments, in combination with the children's interest in combs and combing both their own and the teachers' hair, prompted the teachers to turn to hair.

Investigating Hair

Heather invited the children to accompany her when she went for a haircut at a local salon. The stylist was so pleased by the children's visit that she and her partner closed the shop for the morning so the children could explore the surroundings. The 2- and 3-year-olds tried out the chair that goes around and around and up and down, caught Heather's hair as it fell to the floor, and sat down and drew what they saw. The teachers took photographs, and later made documentation panels about the trip for the children to revisit. The group also made a book of photos, drawings, and children's comments as a thank-you gift for the salon staff.

A hairstylist was also invited to visit the classroom. Parents gave permission for a lock of their child's hair to be snipped; some even gave permission for a full trim. Arthur was nervous before his turn, but after the first snip was made, he smiled and said, "Oh." The locks of hair were laminated on index cards labeled with the child's name on the back. The cards were assembled into a little book so the children could find their own hair and that of their friends and explore the different textures and colors.

Throughout the project, a classroom table had been set aside as a place for investigating faces. There children could draw, look in mirrors, or experiment with changing the facial features on their dolls. Now the teachers put out the hairpieces, which Rhonda had provided in many colors, lengths, and textures. In selecting hair for their dolls, some children matched their own hair, others wanted something different. The children arranged and glued hair as they saw fit. David commented,

> "Now he's a boy, 'cause he has short hair. I have short hair, and I'm a boy."

One girl found a piece of string and wanted a ponytail for her doll. Suddenly many children wanted ponytails, and the teachers provided appropriate materials at the project table.

In observing the play, the teachers noted that when they put a three-sided mirror on the playdough table, children began making faces in it—wrinkling noses, pulling on lips. Two children put playdough over their faces, making molds of their cheeks, noses, and lips. One child, pulling off the playdough mask, said, "See, that's my nose in there."

The teachers extended this interest by having a college student with an arts background make a mask of Heather's face. When Heather's eyes were behind the mask, the children said, "Good-bye" and "We can't see you anymore." Heather thinks they realized that she could not see them, an interesting shift in perspective for the children.

Soon the children pointed out that their dolls could not speak because they didn't have mouths:

> "Heather, my doll wants to kiss you but she has no lips."
> "My doll can't talk. Where's his mouth?"

Such comments were cues for the teachers to move on.

Turning to Noses and Mouths

Since smell and taste are closely allied, the teachers decided to explore noses and mouths together. They planned many activities, including taking shopping trips; baking gingerbread people, bread, and pizza; and preparing fruit salad and homemade ice cream.

Susan took photos of the children's noses and mouths. These were displayed, and teachers invited the children to find their own and their friends' noses and mouths. By this time the children were drawing faces repeatedly.

Teachers brought out the bags of noses and mouths in different colors and shapes (long and skinny, round and full), and the children chose the ones they wanted for their dolls and glued them on. Ian used his doll's nose for a belly button.

A few children then complained that the dolls had no clothes: "My baby's cold." Rhonda supplied a selection of simple clothes (dresses and pants) and many loose pieces of fabric (for sashes, bandanas, shawls, sarongs). The children dressed their dolls during small-group sessions:

> "I put clothes on; she feels happy."
>
> "Maybe there are skirts?"
>
> "My dolly's name is Edward, and he's warm and he feels nice in his clothes."
>
> "Girls have to have dresses because that's what they wear sometimes."

The number of children's drawings of people expanded exponentially. In April Julia's drawing of a woman was accompanied by an extended verbal description (see the middle drawing to the right).

"Round. Shoes here. That's her chin. Here's ears right here. There's a scarf, here we go. Nose, has nose. What else, Joelle? She has a ponytail on it. And has a button on it."

Making Beds for the Dolls

The children often put their dolls to bed, using anything at hand—a shelf, a scarf. The observant teachers planned a visit to a local hotel, where staff invited the children to take a bed apart to see all the items used to make one up: bedspread, blanket, top sheet, bottom sheet, mattress pad. The children even investigated the box springs. They tried out the beds, getting in and out, and jumping on them (not a concern to the hotel employee). They also explored the contents of the hotel room. They climbed under the bed. One child said, "How does the mattress hold?" Children sat and drew what was interesting to them. One 3-year-old chose to draw a flag, spotted when he looked out the window.

The children brought shoe boxes from home to make beds for their dolls. Their interest began to fade naturally once the dolls were put in their beds. With the program year ending, the teachers began wondering how to put the project itself to bed. Finally they held a party, at which the children, families, teachers, and dolls sat together for a celebratory meal, saying good-bye to everyone. The dolls, along with their clothes and beds, went home with the children.

Reflections

Because the teachers were not familiar with emergent curriculum at the beginning of the doll project, they experienced considerable apprehension. The idea of projects was not new to them, but undertaking one was. "We weren't sure what we were doing," admits Joelle, "so it was a learning process for everyone." Their inexperience was an advantage in some ways; it allowed them to take each step slowly and to observe children's responses carefully. Gradually they created new possibilities for curriculum. "We all found it exciting," says Bobbi.

Many interconnecting threads were woven together during the six-month project. Most critical to the project's success was the commitment of the teachers. Susan notes that organization was essential in keeping the content going and the interest level up. In weekly planning meetings the teachers brainstormed possibilities, developed questions to ask the children, and thought about probable responses.

It wasn't easy, though. When planning is responsive rather than programmed, teachers cannot decide what comes next until they see the children's responses and interests and then collaborate on devising a plan to suit them. A responsive approach can create a climate of uncertainty. Yet uncertainty, like conflict, is a characteristic of professional practice (Schön 1983, 1987).

Because of their differing teaching styles, the teachers sometimes disagreed about what to do. Reaching consensus is hard work. Joelle notes, however, "We made compromises and were very professional about that." There is always more to do than reasonably possible, and scheduling conflicts are inherent (e.g., "Should we work on documentation in the morning, when just a few children are present, or should we give them our complete attention?"). For any teacher, juggling multiple demands on her time creates fatigue. All three of these teachers felt that the doll project just about absorbed their entire lives for six months.

Support for the Project

According to Susan, for an emergent curriculum to succeed, "a great deal of support is needed outside the classroom, because of the time constraints for the teachers. The transcriptions alone took ages." Having someone like Susan, who could work on the details of organizing documentation processes and assemble the finished panels, was essential. The documentation panels consisted of texts of children's conversations, photographs, and drawings. Susan says the panels show to others the path of the curriculum; they make learning visible. The fact that the documentation panels were completed by one of the program's directors validated the teachers' work, offering it in visible form to families and other teachers in the center. Although time consuming to construct, panels are an informative, dramatic, and thought-provoking tool for teacher reflection; they help carry a project forward.

The teachers appreciated Barb's implicit support of the project and her appreciation of the results. They also were indebted to Rhonda for her invaluable contributions. The support of the community buoyed the teachers, too. When Joelle first proposed the field trip to a hotel to investigate beds, the other teachers' reaction was, "They won't let us come." But when the community's response was positive, like the salon closing for the children's in-depth hair exploration, Joelle's confidence was rewarded. Now, she says, she is willing to call anyplace and ask whether the center's children might visit.

Finally, as parents became excited about the project, the teachers were affirmed.

Children's Development

Heather believes the children's drawings showed their development in significant ways. Because the topic was so close to the children's deep interests, "it made their representations really meaningful, both to them and to us." She thinks their emotional involvement fostered much more elaborate representations than are typically seen in this age group. The teachers encouraged these representations by keeping drawing materials at hand and by sitting and chatting with the children as they drew.

According to Bobbi, the children experienced a deep focus through revisiting conversations and activities over and over to peel back further layers of thinking and learning. Carol Anne suggests that providing a doll for each child created a focal point for making each child's thinking, desires, and experiences visible. This was particularly helpful because 2- and 3-year-olds are not yet fully verbal.

The children's actions with the dolls and their conversations about them showed teachers what the children were noticing and what they desired. In this way the dolls themselves became a form of documentation that the teachers could "read" in deciding what to plan next. Carol Anne thinks the project's power came in part from the children's identifying with their dolls, as one identifies with an important character in a book. Such empathy results in deeply meaningful events for children.

Because the interactions with the community were so profound, Joelle sees the outings as the most valuable aspect of the project. "Not only did the children grow, but so did the community: They just opened up to us," she says. The staff at the hair salon, optometrist's office, and hotel were delighted with the children's visits and expressed surprise at the toddlers' questions and genuine interest. According to the teachers, the adults in these workplaces came to see the children as thinking people like themselves, rather than merely as cute little kids. The teachers also believe the community considered them more professional after seeing them supporting children's interests. Heather explains, "For the children it's serious: They're investigating the world, and we're enhancing that. Going into the community made us look a lot more professional."

Teacher Development

As the project progressed month by month, Barb, Susan, and the teachers in the other rooms noticed that the decision making of the teachers involved in the doll project became more assured, creative, and inspired.

The images Heather, Joelle, and Bobbi had of themselves as teachers altered during the project. Joelle's language use with children changed considerably. She learned to provide a running commentary on children's actions ("You're putting your eyes on the doll's tummy") rather than telling children what to do ("Put the eyes on the face"). She came to realize that describing back their actions to the children is better for their decision making, and this realization helped her slow down to observe children's responses more carefully.

Witnessing the children's development and interest in representational skills opened the teachers' eyes to children's potential. And it reinforced Bobbi's belief in arts-based learning. She realized that 2- and 3-year-olds could understand much more about their bodies than she had thought:

> "I didn't know that, developmentally, children of 2 and 3 could do this. I thought children in [Reggio Emilia] Italy must be extremely intelligent—they must have pencils in the womb. I didn't know children here could do that."

Heather believes that teachers naturally try to provide children with "the best that you know." But in the press of daily classroom life, she says, teachers worry about "stagnating, not looking for things for yourself as a teacher." Heather adds, "Not that we were doing anything bad [before the project], but we just weren't using our potential." The teachers felt they would do such a project again, because they learned so much from it. Heather thinks she would focus on small-group rather than whole-group involvement. Bobbi thinks she would concentrate on more thought-provoking questions.

As Bobbi says, "The doll project not only permitted us to teach children but also showed parents and the community what children can do. The project put the meaning back in the word *teacher*."

Laurie Kocher and
Veronica Pacini-Ketchabaw

Quality Is Found in the Here and Now of Practice

Through our own experiences working with children, families, and teachers, we have become aware that pedagogy is indeed, as curriculum theorist William Pinar (2008) reminds us, a "complicated conversation." We have witnessed a tendency to think of early childhood practice as a simple matter that can be easily prescribed and directly applied. Clearly the teachers involved with The Doll Project discover that teaching can be much more complicated and enriching, both for themselves and for the children. In this brief reflection, we consider The Doll Project, the thoughts of pedagogues and teachers in Reggio Emilia, and our own experiences working with teachers in British Columbia, Canada.

What Emerges From Listening to Children

In The Doll Project, these responsive teachers *listen* to the children's interests by paying close attention to the play they observe with the classroom dolls. In *answering* the children, they offer them featureless cloth dolls. By doing so, they step out of a comfort zone of predetermined curriculum and venture forth into emergent work. Although it can be a little unsettling to work in unfamiliar ways, such a "pedagogy of listening" embraces what Carla Rinaldi describes as "a context in which children's curiosity, theories, and research are legitimated and listened to, a context in which children feel comfortable and confident, motivated and respected" (Rinaldi 2006, 126).

We see early childhood settings as spaces for children, families, teachers, and communities to engage and interact, opening up dynamic possibilities for program quality. Quality isn't located somewhere "out there"—it is found in the here and now of each teacher's everyday practice, as is in The Doll Project. In this way, quality emerges as a response to local circumstances and interactions (Pacini-Ketchabaw et al., forthcoming). As teachers step into unfamiliar terrain, we find that the complex questions that emerge in discussions highlight early childhood pedagogies as "inherently relational, emergent, and nonlinear process[es] that . . . [are] . . . unpredictable and therefore unknowable in advance" (Sellar 2009, 351).

The Power of Pedagogical Documentation

Documentation, as understood in early childhood practices, draws inspiration from the Reggio Emilia experience. Photos, videos, audio recordings, and scribed conversations are gathered as research traces of children's explorations. This documentation is studied closely by the teachers. When the teachers add their reflections and ideas into the mix, it then becomes *pedagogical documentation*. A key component of pedagogical documentation then involves making these ideas visible through a variety of means, including wall panels, booklets, short videos, or PowerPoint-style presentations.

Pedagogical documentation or, as we have come to call it, pedagogical narration, can be a tool for critical reflection, planning, and action within a discourse of meaning making. Reviewing and discussing documentation allows teachers to collaborate while provoking, stretching, and challenging each other's thinking in relation to theories and practices. The contingencies, uncertainties, and complexities of practice emerge through their intensive discussions. By making children's learning visible, children become active learners, teachers value the roles of community and relationships in learning, and curriculum emerges as an experiential, dynamic, and relational process.

The Importance of Involving Community Members

An unexpected result of The Doll Project is the enthusiastic and profound support of community members, contributing to a shifting image of both children and teachers. Pedagogical documentation can make the everyday learning experiences and practices of the early childhood classroom visible and open to engagement, discussion and debate, and co-construction with families and the wider community.

Through the participation of families and other community members, the child and the early learning classroom are situated in relationship to the community and are viewed as contributing to understanding the particularities of the local context (Kocher 2010; Moss 2007).

Pedagogical documentation, then, serves an important advocacy role in communicating that children are respected citizens and that early learning spaces house important activities. Community members who encounter and engage with The Doll Project see that early childhood teachers are not simply observers and guides, caretakers and technicians. Teachers' complex practices with children, families, and colleagues are made visible to the community.

An Image of the Competent Child

Educators from Reggio Emilia challenge us to change our image of the child from one who is needy and requires intervention, to a child who is rich in competencies and full of potential (Rinaldi 2006). The Doll Project teachers see the children as co-constructors of meaning and the adults as facilitators who provide opportunities for learning. In this approach, teachers look for practical ways to develop curriculum that responds to children's interests, recognizes their competencies, and honors the children's voices.

We see the image of the child as continually emerging through teachers' practices, as was the case in The Doll Project. The image teachers hold is not fixed, but is always shifting, always in the process of becoming something new and different.

The Complexities of Competent Teachers

Early childhood practice is a complex journey, and as such it requires an understanding of the complex roles played by teachers. In Reggio Emilia, teachers do not simply guide and observe children, nor do they follow a prescribed curriculum. They seek ways to extend children's learning and engagement, and they make children's theories and ideas visible through pedagogical documentation. In these ways, the early childhood teacher is positioned as a researcher. As Vecchi (1998) describes, the teacher/researcher uses pedagogical documentation as "an indispensable source to be able to 'read' and reflect critically . . . on the experience we are living, the projects we are exploring. This allows us to construct theories and hypotheses that are not arbitrarily or artificially imposed on the children" (pp. 141–42).

This notion of researcher is strongly reflected in The Doll Project. Readers of pedagogical documentation view early childhood teachers as more than technicians, custodians, experts, or maternal substitutes. Rather, these teachers are open to the unexpected and to learning that is "impossible to predict, plan, supervise or evaluate according to predefined standards" (Olsson 2009, 117).

Conversations such as these, while challenging, serve to complexify teaching practices and contribute to the teachers' intellectual engagement with their work.

Complexifying Practice

In closing, we see in The Doll Project an engagement with what we call *complexifying practices*. We view complexifying practice as an incomplete, ongoing, messy process filled with struggles, tensions, challenges, frustrations, unknowns, discomfort, and divergences in positions. At the same time, within these spaces deep connections are created, and "lines of flight" that crack open pre-established modes of thinking and acting tend to emerge. The Doll Project teachers do this by questioning assumptions about what young children know and what they can do. They question what counts as appropriate practice, what their roles as early childhood educators are, and what those roles could be. They question how they view families and examine many other aspects of their work. Their thinking and practices shift as a result of their openness to discuss, stretch their thinking, and move beyond the constraints of their own perspectives.

....

Laurie Kocher, PhD, is an instructor in the early childhood education program at Douglas College near Vancouver, BC. Her academic research has focused on the pedagogical documentation practices of Reggio Emilia.

Veronica Pacini-Ketchabaw, PhD, is associate professor and coordinator of the early years specialization, and co-director of the Unit for Early Years Research and Development, at the School of Child and Youth Care, University of Victoria, British Columbia.

Chapter 6

**Valerie Quann and
Carol Anne Wien**

The Visible Empathy of Infants and Toddlers

Katherine, 8 months old, sits on the carpet in the middle of a bustling child care room. She has been mesmerized by a pop-up toy but glances up during her play and seems frightened by the commotion around her. Brandon, 19 months old, who sits nearby, notices her change in mood. Katherine begins to cry. Brandon toddles toward her and gently leans over to whisper in her ear. He babbles to her in an unmistakable "motherese" tone, seeming to convey "Don't worry" while also gently patting her hand. He comforts her in the same way the teachers comfort the children.

Do infants and toddlers really show empathy? What does it look like? Can empathy be documented in very young children who have limited language skills? Can educators discern any factors that enable empathy to develop in infants and toddlers?

Our purpose here is to invite conversation among practitioners, teacher educators, and scholars on empathy in young children. We write as teacher educators whose work involves the professional preparation of early childhood and elementary teachers. We describe what Valerie Quann observed in a multiage setting, what we make of these observations grounded in qualitative research, and our reflections. We do not try to tell others what to do, but rather we ask, What do you think about the possibility of the very young in your setting showing empathy? Do other practitioners see anything like these episodes? What do empathy researchers think about what we are seeing? And in what ways can we consider the cultivation of empathy an aspect of emergent curriculum?

The Setting

Valerie had worked in an urban child care environment in which 58 children from 3 months to 6 years of age were organized into four classrooms, one of which was multiage. The program, a lab school in a university setting, served a culturally diverse population with many families from professional backgrounds. In her work, she had noticed that very young children seemed fine-tuned to one another's feelings and able to put themselves emotionally in the position of others long before researchers in moral reasoning expect to observe empathy (Damon 1988; Kohlberg 1969; Piaget [1932] 1965).

Definitions of Empathy

We define *empathy* in very young children as the capacity to observe the feelings of another and to respond with care and concern for that other, noting Hendrick & Weissman's definition of empathy as "kindness toward another when there is a perceived or real sadness about that person. This [showing kindness] is a difficult task because young children are essentially centered on themselves and have great difficulty grasping how others feel" (2010, 223). We argue, in contrast, that teachers do see remarkable incidents of empathy among very young children. Noddings (2003, 30) offers the notion of empathy as "feeling with" the other; we agree that there is a mutuality of feeling offered by one person to another.

We acknowledge the psychological literature on empathy, altruism, and prosocial development (Damon 1988; Eisenberg 1986, 1992; Hoffman 2000; Sroufe 1996) and offer our teacher research as a counterpoint that shows what practitioners observe and experience. In doing so, we recall Loris Malaguzzi describing how Reggio educators believe that learning about children could happen first and foremost from observing children themselves: "Indeed, education without research or innovation is education without interest" (Malaguzzi 1998, 73).

We want to ask what others think about what we have found.

Pedagogical Documentation

This chapter was first published in the July 2006 issue of *Young Children*.

Pedagogical documentation is a form of teacher research inspired by the educators of Reggio Emilia. It uses photographs of children at work, samples of their efforts, and text—children's conversations, teachers' thoughts—to show to those outside of classrooms the intriguing events occurring inside classrooms for young children (Cadwell 2003; Dahlberg, Moss, & Pence 2007; Giudici, Rinaldi, & Krechevsky 2001). We believed that by documenting these events for those outside classroom life, we could show the empathy of infants and toddlers. These are episodes so evanescent that their duration is a matter of seconds or minutes; they are events that can be missed altogether if adults are not alert to them.

At the lab school where she had worked, Valerie observed the infant and toddler classroom (eight children, ages 6 months to 2½ years) and the multiage group (13 children, ages 2½ to 4 years), which joined together for substantial parts of the day. Each observation lasted about three hours. They took place on nine occasions over 10 weeks. Watching for episodes of empathy, she photographed and took careful notes when discerning an event that seemed to fit our definition. She documented 13 episodes, from a brief flashing moment to an extended period of several minutes. Valerie made seven sets of documentation panels with photographs and descriptions to share with the classroom teachers in a collaborative reflection on what was occurring.

Three Forms of Empathy

We saw three types of empathy in her pedagogical documentation, which Carol Anne Wien defines as follows. *Proximal empathy* occurs when a child shows concerned care for a distressed classmate who is close by, though not having been involved in the classmate's upset. *Altruistic empathy* occurs when a child offers concerned care in response to another child's suffering by noticing it from afar. *Self-corrective empathy* occurs when a child offers concerned care in response to his or her own actions having caused distress to another.

Proximal Empathy

In a show of proximal empathy, a child responds with care and concern to a nearby child who is hurt. In Valerie's observations, this usually occurred when two children were playing in a learning center together. The responding child did not cause nor have anything to do with the other child's being hurt or upset, but was nearby and decided to help in his or her own way, usually with kind words or touching, as in the following example.

> Destiny (23 months) and Pratha (20 months) play in the creative area, attempting to make scissors cut paper. Destiny, who has not had much experience using scissors, struggles to hold them. As she struggles, her index finger bends backward and she begins to cry. Pratha says, "Ouch," and touches Destiny's hand. Pratha then looks up, presumably for a teacher. Teacher Leona comes over with ice and comforts Destiny. Pratha stands nearby with a concerned look on her face.

In proximal empathy, a child becomes aware of and responds to another child's suffering because he or she is close by. In this instance, Pratha seems to "feel with" Destiny, acknowledging her hurt and wanting her to feel better.

It seems that some children become upset when other children are visibly upset. Our inference is that even infants and toddlers "catch" the feeling of distress and respond, perhaps because of their relationship with the upset child, perhaps out of shared knowledge of what it feels like to be upset, or perhaps out of a global emotional tone for the situation. It is as if the child who witnesses the hurt wants to communicate her acknowledgment of the hurt.

> Wyatt (2½ years) has fallen on the carpet, and it quickly becomes clear that he is injured. A teacher comforts him. Amanda (17 months) goes to the small fridge in the

room and retrieves an ice pack. She brings it over to Wyatt. Her face says, "There," as she puts the ice beside him and "All better now" as she turns and walks away. She is smiling.

Many children in this classroom attempt to show care for their upset peers by bringing them ice. Perhaps the children remember that when they were hurt, the teachers brought them ice and then they felt better. One time a child brought another child ice when he was crying due to morning separation from his parent. The upset child accepted the ice and, very soon after, stopped crying. In this environment, it was as if ice represents a gift of caring, of compassion: To be offered ice is to be healed.

Altruistic Empathy

In altruistic empathy, a child notices distress from much farther away, when involved in a different activity that might preclude attention to the distress of another. In altruistic empathy, there seems to be attunement to the distress of others and a concerted desire to assuage it.

Matthew (22 months) is out of sorts today, crying at the gate at the classroom door, wanting to leave (presumably to go after his mother, who left about an hour earlier). Two teachers have tried to comfort and distract him, but he remains upset. Amanda (17 months) brings him several trains; everyone knows they are his favorite toy. He throws them over the gate. One teacher successfully redirects him to a puzzle. Later, the other teacher picks up the trains and returns them to their bin.

Amanda peers into the bins. She looks around the room, and when she sees Matthew, her face lights up. She brings the trains over and silently puts them on the table beside him. Colin (17 months) walks by the table, picks up the trains, and walks away. Matthew cries out and begins to chase Colin. Mathew moves to a corner, crying loudly, and throws several toys. He has a large bell in his hand as Amanda approaches with another train she has found; she offers it to him. He puts the bell down, takes the train, and sits on the carpet, holding it. Amanda returns to reading books with Emma and a student teacher. Matthew puts down the train, goes to a bookshelf, picks out a book, and joins them. He is much happier for the rest of the morning.

As the teachers noticed when reviewing the documentation panel with Valerie, Amanda's solution is more fine-tuned than their own: She "knows" exactly what will please Matthew—his favorite toy. When Colin walks off with her offer of comfort, Matthew becomes enraged and loses all control. Amanda hangs in, finding another train and offering it once again. It is as if she assures Matthew that he will be comforted, as if she has a sort of persistence in seeing him through his upset. We might infer that while the teachers clearly make many different attempts to console this child, a young child in their midst joins them and also makes repeated attempts. Altruistic empathy is kindness in which a child interrupts her own activity and goes out of her way to show care for another person.

Extended Altruistic Empathy

A single child reacted in a thoughtful and striking manner toward another's hurt when a roomful of other children did not notice the problem. Amanda displayed empathy for other children's suffering when she was not only not involved in the cause but often busy playing in another part of the room. If she noticed that another child "needed care" of some kind, she would often leave what she was doing to go to that child and offer help.

Wyatt (2½ years) sits in a low, wheeled cart that allows him mobility after having broken his leg. He tries to maneuver around the room, but his cart gets stuck on the leg of the sand table. Amanda (17 months) is on the other side of the room reading a book. She glances up and notices Wyatt gesturing and making sounds. She leaves her book on the carpet and walks over to Wyatt. She leans over and looks in his eyes. It looks like she is saying, "Don't worry, we'll figure this out." Wyatt smiles at her.

Amanda tries to move the cart back and forth but cannot make it move. She tries to push the book shelf on the other side of the cart, but it is too heavy. Then she tries to push the sand table aside and is successful. Wyatt points to the bookshelf and Amanda moves his cart in that direction. Wyatt uses his hands to move the wheels on his chair so Amanda needs to help him only minimally. Together the children move to the bookshelf.

Amanda waits while Wyatt searches the shelf. He reaches with his arm toward *Goodnight Moon* and Amanda waits, as if to see whether he can reach it. When she realizes that he cannot, she moves the book closer to him so that he can grasp it on his own. Wyatt takes the book but looks distressed when he realizes that he cannot move his wheels with the book in his hand. He looks at Amanda, and she accepts the book from him. Wyatt points to the carpet area, indicating that he would like to go there. Amanda holds the book in her hand and pushes Wyatt to the carpet area. She smiles and goes back to her spot on the carpet.

Even at her young age, Amanda shows what we consider a deep sense of empathy, in that she seems to put herself in the place of others, to grasp their needs, even when she is not directly involved in the situation. In the midst of another activity, she spots others in need. As we watch her reactions while helping—her smiles and appearance of satisfaction—we infer helping others in need is deeply satisfying to her.

Self-Corrective Empathy

Self-corrective empathy occurs when a child is the cause of another child's hurt feelings or injury. In response to the resulting suffering, the perpetrator shows empathy toward the hurt child. The following example shows how this works.

> Michael, a 4-year-old preschooler in this multiage classroom, is putting spools on a string to make a necklace. He is quietly working alone when Amanda approaches and starts to play with the end of his string. With her other hand, she reaches for a red wooden ring. Michael yells, "No! Go away." He pulls the string out of Amanda's hands.
>
> Amanda's face crumples, as though she might cry, yet she still tries to grab the string.
>
> Michael then puts some beads near her and says, "Here, these are for you." They work silently, with Amanda watching Michael string his spools onto the string as she does the same. He glances over at her and notices her watching him. He smiles and says, "Look, you're doing it."

Michael first reacts harshly, protecting his activity from interference. When he sees Amanda start to cry, he stops and seems to rethink his reaction. In fact, he changes his response from a harsh rejection to an offer of material that enables Amanda to join his activity. We believe that this is a sophisticated empathic behavior. At first, Michael reacts egocentrically, protecting something he sees as his. Yet, following Amanda's hurt, nonverbal reaction, he invites her into his activity. Essentially, he switches his mindset from exclusion to inclusion. We think this a profoundly moving response, for even in adulthood it is difficult to change one's behavior midstream to be more tolerant, more inclusive.

Hoffman (2000, 114) discusses empathy-based guilt, a painful feeling of loss of esteem for oneself, "usually accompanied by a sense of urgency, tension, and regret that results from empathic feeling for someone in distress, combined with awareness of being the cause of that distress." We are not sure we want to infer that children so young are reacting out of guilt: What is clear is the successful switch in response in the midst of emotion. We find this switch powerful, because it suggests that positive care for others is strong enough to stop one's negative reaction to another person.

Hoffman noted in his research that as 2-year-olds, children show "more aggression and more pleasure in the victim's distress when they caused the other's distress than when they witnessed it. . . . In any case, causing another's distress is more likely to require adult intervention than witnessing another's distress" (2000, 136). Michael's reaction is even more surprising, given Hoffman's suggestion that episodes such as this generally result in more adult intervention. Michael, a preschooler, was able to regulate his own behavior and did not draw adult attention or intervention. We consider his response a highly sophisticated communication.

Discussion Among the Teachers

When Valerie discussed these episodes with the classroom teachers, Kathleen and Leona, they perceived Amanda's behavior to be altruistic—in their view, offered without a notion of gain for herself. Kathleen said, "[Amanda] seems to be completely empathic in an altruistic sense. . . . She's not trying to make up for something she's done or make it better when she's hurt somebody."

Damon (1988) argues,

> Newborns have the capacity for some purely affective empathic responses. These early feelings become the emotional cornerstone of prosocial behavior. But for effective moral action, the child must learn to identify a wide range of emotional states in others. Further, the child

must acquire the ability to anticipate what kinds of action will improve the emotional state of the other. (p. 15)

What is so striking about Amanda's day-to-day behavior is that she does seem to enact what Damon calls "effective moral action." Amanda displayed this knowledge especially well in the episode with Wyatt and his cart. She seemed to know intuitively that Wyatt needed only a small bit of help to meet his goal. Some adults might have taken over, pushing him where he needed to go and retrieving the book for him. But Amanda offered him scaffolded support; she moved the book over just so far so that Wyatt could reach it. She allowed him to push his cart with his hands on the wheels, and she pushed only that small amount extra that enabled him to be successful. Her actions imply that she understood the wide range of emotional states that Damon discusses: She seems to understand Wyatt's need to participate and also the limits of his ability to do so.

Can a Child Be Too Empathetic?

It is legitimate to ask whether Amanda is too empathic, interrupting her own activity to offer care to others. Valerie struggled with this, thinking she didn't want Amanda to stop being empathic, yet didn't want her needs to be forgotten either. Hoffman (2000) argues that it can be typical in later schooling for girls who are very agreeable to have their needs overlooked for others who seem needier.

Carol Anne argues that Amanda's successful acts to restore positive emotion in others do in fact satisfy a need in her—perhaps for harmony of relations or for restoring others to equanimity—and that her success supports her sense of personal power and efficacy, as seen by her smiles, even though she is not yet 20 months old. Batson and Shaw (1991) would seem to agree with Carol Anne's interpretations of these events:

Altruism and egoism . . . have much in common. Each refers to goal-directed motivation; each is concerned with the ultimate goal of this motivation; and for each, the ultimate goal is increasing someone's welfare. These common features provide the context for highlighting the crucial difference: Whose welfare is the ultimate goal—another person's or one's own? (p. 108)

How Is Empathy Generated?

What conditions encourage empathy for others? The explanation for the empathy shown by the children in this child care setting, we believe, is the high quality of adult-child relationships and interactions modeled by the teachers and adult family members. This school holds relationships at the heart of its program. Forming and sustaining positive relationships is the first priority, as teachers engage children in meaningful ways and form authentic, lasting relationships with families. Leona said,

"You have to work hard at a real relationship with the family. If there are problems, we work at them. Hard. We respect differences in parenting styles. You could be working with this family for five years. It's a real relationship and we need to treat it like that."

Eisenberg (1992, 112) comments, "It seems obvious that teachers and peers must influence children's prosocial development. Once children enter school, they spend a large amount of time with teachers and friends." In a child care setting, children can spend up to 10 hours a day together. This is bound to affect their behavior in terms of learning from what they see and experience.

Kathleen and Leona, the teachers in this multiage classroom, said they strongly believe in using appropriate, positive language. Kathleen also thought that the children learned much through modeling. Leona agreed that the children saw others acting and reacting in a particular way and then learned from that observation. Leona helped children negotiate their boundaries by encouraging them to verbalize their feelings through language. Both teachers would guide less verbal children by providing them with appropriate language choices, saying such things as,

"You are crying. That looks like it really hurt when you were pushed. What could you say to Aidan?"

If the child was not verbal, the teacher would continue,

"You could try saying 'Stop' or 'That hurts.'"

The teachers also recognized the importance of nonverbal communication. They taught the children American Sign Language signs for *stop, help,* and *more,* among other needs, to enhance their independence and to help them feel more self-control during peer interactions. In addition, surrounding the teachers' positive language was an aura of emotional regard for every participant in the setting—children, teachers, and families. This aura of emotional support included body language, voice tone and inflection, and a stance of caring that became infectious and was caught by others in the setting.

Reflections

We believe the relationship between teachers and children is the most important factor influencing how children act within any type of early learning setting. Without the high-quality relationships that Valerie observed, we suspect little empathy would have occurred in this setting. What we saw suggests three ways in particular that teachers and administrators might encourage children to be empathic.

Create a Culture of Caring

The teachers Valerie observed always spoke in an authentic way, using natural language in a conversational manner, with respect for each child, engaging the children and responding to their needs. When children observe teachers and older children behaving in this way, they catch the feeling and also pass it on. Helping children understand the feelings of others is an integral aspect of the curriculum of living together. The relationships among teachers, between children and teachers, and among children are fostered with warm and caring interactions.

A child cannot be spoiled by being loved and respected or by learning how to love and respect others.

Document Prosocial Behavior

Closely observing the children and constructing documentation panels greatly helped Valerie to understand what was occurring in the classroom. After each panel was created, Valerie met with the teachers to reflect on what had occurred in the classroom. This always brought out rich discussion and deeper reflection on the classroom experience. Then the panels were posted, so that the children could also observe and revisit their experiences with help from the teachers.

When teachers carefully observe children for empathy and other positive social-emotional behaviors, and document those behaviors for others to see, they highlight the importance of constructing positive social-emotional spaces for living. In uncertain and turbulent times, we consider such values a basic right and necessity for children.

Allow Unhurried Time

The episode in which Amanda helped Wyatt navigate between his needs and his limits in their early childhood setting is an example of the benefits that occur when teachers allow expansive time frames for activity. When Wyatt was first stuck at the sand table, a teacher could have just reached over and tapped the table aside so that he could get through. However, Valerie and the teachers waited to observe what might occur.

Amanda came quickly to Wyatt's aid and gave him the help he needed to move throughout the room. Because the adults waited, Wyatt was empowered to move himself with a small amount of help, and Amanda was allowed to practice empathic behavior. It is this type of keen observation and respectful interaction by the teachers that permits children higher degrees of participation in deciding what to do and allows us to see the remarkable empathic reciprocity that even infants and toddlers seem capable of showing.

Finally, in what ways do stories of empathy show aspects of emergent curriculum? Carol Anne sees three aspects to highlight, and they show the close connection between developmentally appropriate practice and its opening out into practices that allow emergence. The keystone, in her view, is that the adults are looking for—and expecting to see—the competencies of children (Rinaldi 2006). Stances that are based in managing children efficiently can overlook children's capability because it is not on the agenda. Stances based in searching merely for developmental norms might overlook empathy because it is not expected to be seen. It is the openness to observing children as they are, not as they have been theorized or imagined to be, and to observing with an appreciation for their capability, intelligence, and resourcefulness, that allows us to see with fresh eyes (Rinaldi 2006). One way this capability emerges is in altering the lens by which we observe so that we are attentive to the connections and attachments children are making in relation to their environment. A second way this capability emerges is in the capacity of the adults *not* to step in to assist immediately, but rather to suspend their response long enough to allow openings that permit the child to take action.

A third aspect is the fine-grained observation and documentation undertaken by Valerie and her construction of panels for study and interpretation. It is the *study* of documentation that allows it to become pedagogical, for we see things we had not seen before: It teaches us.

What emerged here was adult awareness of young children's empathy, a quality of emotion and moral acts of caring both unexpected and beautiful to witness.

Mary Benson
McMullen

The Legacy of *Visible Empathy*: Teaching Us to Be More "Care-Aware"

C arol Anne Wien and Valerie Quann invited us into an important conversation in their marvelous chapter, asking readers to consider not whether infants and toddlers are capable of empathy, but **what educators can do** to help very young children develop empathy. Valerie and Carol Anne add to the existing research on empathy and altruism by identifying three forms of empathy in infants and toddlers—proximal, altruistic, and self-corrective empathy. They provide language to guide observations, giving us a framework for documenting empathy and validating that very young children are capable of exhibiting this complex emotion.

As early childhood professionals, the social-emotional development of young children is at the heart and soul of our practice, especially with children birth to age 3; it is core to our philosophy as early childhood educators. As increased numbers of infants and toddlers are cared for by non-family members outside of the home, researchers, teacher educators, parents, and practitioners seek ways to ensure their healthy overall psychological and physical well-being now and for the rest of their lives.

There is, however, a growing sense of urgency to focus more deliberately on specific aspects of "care" and "caring" in early childhood **care** and education. This results in an increased focus on the psychological and emotional components of well-being. Educators wish to instill in children a love of self and respect and compassion for others. At the same time we are increasingly motivated to focus on fostering prosocial development because we are troubled by bullying in our schools, a lack of civility in our workplaces and politics, and violent acts to which we are exposed too frequently in the news.

Like Valerie and Carol Anne, Gordon (2005) presents empathy as something to work on very purposefully with infants and toddlers, calling it essential in education and parenting if we seek a better world. She writes passionately about how empathy results from the loving relationships babies have, saying, "Love grows brains" (p. 18). She cites research linking empathy to critical thinking skills, creativity, moral reasoning, and problem solving, all important academic skills, of course, but also very important in helping people become psychologically and emotionally intelligent as well.

In my own research about infants and toddlers in child care, I have witnessed the power of the suggestions made by Valerie and Carol Anne in this chapter. I have experienced the results when unhurried time is allowed, relationships and interactions thrive, and positive caring skills and problem-solving behaviors are practiced and nurtured. I have reviewed teachers' documentation of prosocial behavior, and observed teachers partnering effectively with families around mutually agreed on goals. And, I have found when cultures of caring surround infants and toddlers there is positive impact on the well-being of everyone involved—teachers, children, families, and administrators.

Unfortunately, I have also witnessed firsthand what happens in environments in which care is not the central focus and prosocial development is actively, if unintentionally, discouraged. I describe fully my experiences in relationship-based infant and toddler environments that foster prosocial skills such as empathy (McMullen et al. 2009) and one that does not (McMullen 2010) in two contrasting articles.

Creating Cultures of Caring

It is important to surround infants and toddlers with positive relationships in what Valerie and Carol Anne call *cultures of care*, including the relationships between and among teachers and families, staff members (teaching and non-teaching), administrators, and all others who interact with the program. To create cultures of care, we must

- Communicate respectfully by remaining fully present and engaged with all of our communication partners, adults and children, and respond appropriately to all communications, verbal and nonverbal
- Respond sensitively, with kindness and compassion to everyone's needs and by meeting those needs in a timely manner
- Value and honor all members of the community by supporting and acknowledging their contributions as important and necessary within the child care community

If these things are done throughout the child care community with all members of that community, from the youngest infant to the most wizened elder, we can create cultures of caring and relating that support the well-being of everyone in the environment, and most importantly, that instill in its youngest members lifelong lessons about what it means to be givers and receivers of care, to be fully human.

Conclusion

The legacy of the Visible Empathy researchers, teacher educators, and practitioners is to take their findings to heart and become more ***care-aware***, by

1. Acknowledging infants and toddlers have the capacity to engage in caring behaviors and to feel concern for self and others

2. Being mindful in our observations of infants and toddlers, noting and responding sensitively to their early empathic, caring responses

3. Understanding infants and toddlers learn they are worthy of being cared for and how to care for others from the actions and behaviors of those around them

4. Engaging in and encouraging practices that allow caring and empathy to flourish and grow among infants and toddlers

5. Being aware of our caring responses to everyone in our environments, children and adults, as we model what it means to live and learn in a culture of care

It is important for educators to seize every opportunity to foster early empathic behaviors in infants and toddlers, such as those described by Valerie and Carol Anne, reinforce prosocial behaviors, and nurture a sense of belonging to a caring community. This is done best within a culture of caring, one that benefits us all, now and well into the future.

....

Mary Benson McMullen, PhD, is professor of early childhood education at Indiana University in Bloomington, Indiana. Her scholarship focuses on issues of caring, sensitive relationships in birth through age 5 child care settings.

Chapter 7

**Carol Anne Wien,
Bobbi-Lynn Keating,
Annette Comeau, and
Barbara Bigelow**

Moving Into Uncertainty: Sculpture With 3- to 5-Year-Olds

"It's not playdough. It's sculpture," said Omar, one January day, when invited to put away the playdough before lunch.

We found his comment intriguing. What could the term *sculpture* mean to this 4-year old? Did any of the other 16 children in the room also think playdough creations were sculpture? The teachers thought Omar's comment was profound, and when teacher Bobbi-Lynn Keating followed up, asking other children what they thought about sculpture, she found there was avid and startling interest.

During the 2005–06 year, Carol Anne Wien visited this classroom weekly as an educational consultant, listening, observing, and meeting with the staff—Bobbi and coteacher Matthew Sampson, center artist/assistant director Annette Comeau, and director Barbara Bigelow. The following week Carol Anne returned to find Omar's comment displayed on the documentation shelf, a place that shows and describes the children's work for families and others. The comment and several photos were accompanied by some lumpish playdough animals—a cat, a turtle.

What do 3- to 5-year-olds know about sculpture? What do they think it is? Where did their ideas come from? How do they differentiate between their usual playdough molding, which gets thrown back into the tub at the end of a session, and sculpture?

Omar's comment launched a six-month emergent curriculum project on sculpture in this child care center inspired by the Reggio Emilia experience (Edwards, Gandini, & Forman 2012; Vecchi et al. 2011). Since 1996 the center has been working to transform its curriculum into one that follows the minds of children—listening alertly to their ideas, desires, and hopes—and supports the children in expanding and developing their theories about the world with strong, purposeful curriculum activities embedded with rich learning. In addition to describing the sculpture project, we trace the thinking behind the decisions that teachers made to support the children's developing ideas.

First Responses

For Bobbi and Matthew, the rash of new playdough animals and the children's insistence they were making sculpture was "this real scary discovery." The fear arose because neither knew anything about sculpture or how to make it, and the idea of embarking on an inquiry into the children's notions felt like "jumping without a net."

For several weeks, the teachers' response was to do more of the same—offer lots more playdough and begin to document what the children did with it. *Pedagogical documentation* is a teacher research process that educators use in Reggio-inspired programs (Edwards, Gandini, & Forman 2012; Vecchi et al. 2011). Such documentation—in this case, taking photographs of children as they worked and noting their comments and conversations— helps to make children's theories and learning visible, both to themselves and to others (Edwards, Gandini, & Forman 2012; Wien, Guyevskey, & Berdoussis 2011).

As a result of this documenting, Bobbi noticed the children's frustration with playdough as a medium: "It won't stay together" . . . "It's breaking." Also, the children wanted to revisit their playdough sculptures to work more on them, but their works dried out and became fragile. The children seemed to hold the implicit notion that if it was sculpture, you kept it.

Problems Open Up a Line of Inquiry

This chapter was first published in the July 2008 issue of *Young Children*.

Bobbi describes emergent curriculum as "like a road" she is on, and she sees a new problem as adding excitement to her work: "The problem gives me a direction." In this case, she went to artist Annette, an expert with materials, to discuss the children's frustrations. Annette thought immediately of potter's clay, but this material also dries out quickly and can be as fragile as playdough. She then suggested modeling clay (e.g., Plasticine). In previous projects, Bobbi had found modeling clay unsuccessful: It was stiff and unyielding, and the children did only the most rudimentary rolling and sticking together with it. Annette suggested it might be more "sculptural" to keep the colors neutral—grays, black, white. This would focus attention on its tactile rather than visual qualities. Bobbi put aside her misgivings and agreed to try it, wondering what would happen.

During some small-group times, when four or five children worked together with a teacher on an activity, Bobbi explored modeling clay with the children. The children responded to it with increased focus on their work. When Bobbi introduced real pottery tools, such as wedges, palette knives, and scribing tools, they experimented with adding details. As they worked daily with the modeling clay, the children's confidence with the material increased, and more and more children attempted ideas with the medium.

Through studying the ongoing documentation, the center staff and Carol Anne saw that many children worked flat, creating their objects in two dimensions, or they attempted three-dimensional pieces without success. It is difficult to get three-dimensional materials to stand tall, and this property troubled the children. For example, five children were entranced by a basket of artificial sunflowers and tried to represent them in modeling clay. Documentation revealed their frustration expressed through comments such as these:

"They are just lying down."

"Why won't they stand up?"

"They won't get up."

Bobbi noticed that the children's struggle to build vertically was constant as they worked with the modeling clay.

The Problem of Vertical Stability

Bobbi wondered whether to demonstrate to the children how to make their work stand upright. Should the teachers show them what an artist might do? Reggio's Loris Malaguzzi talks about adults "loaning" their knowledge to children, but with the expectation that the loan will be "repaid" (Malaguzzi in Gandini 2012). Children might repay the loan by going further with their sculptures than they would be able to without the technical support provided by the adults. How far should the center staff go?

Annette suggested showing the children how an artist might use a wire armature, or framework, for getting a sculpture to stand up in three dimensions. In several small-group times, she wrapped wire first around a rock, as a base, and then loosely vertical, and demonstrated how to add lumps of playdough to the wire and mold it on the armature. The children were enthralled. With their own wire-wrapped rocks, they explored bending the loose wire on top into shapes and adding clumps of gritty playdough (Annette had added coffee grounds to give the playdough a stone-like texture). These materials were highly effective for large-scale three-dimensional work, and soon various children had created a cat, a lizard, and a police dog with a worm on its back.

Sharing Displays With the Children

The teachers displayed six of the rock and wire-supported sculptures on a low shelf, a cloth underneath, with photos of each child working on his or her sculpture. Each was accompanied by a little card with the child artist's name and comment about the work. We found it interesting that even the 3-year-old children understood this arrangement as a display. While the children rearranged the items frequently, showing others the photos and labels and conversing about them, they did not play with the objects. They seemed to treasure the fact that their work was being kept and shown.

Some quality of permanence and visibility seemed central to their implicit notions of sculpture, though we can only hypothesize about the origin of their theories. Four months earlier, a parent who worked at a kiln had donated leftover reclining clay figures. Several of these were on display around the classroom. These figures seemed a probable source for the children's theories, though we cannot be sure. If they were the source, it is an interesting example of the Reggio (and Montessori) notion of the power of the environment itself to teach. The idea is that resources and their organization in the room have the power to compel ideas and actions in children (Malaguzzi in Gandini 2012; Montessori [1912] 1964).

The Children's Evolving Concepts of Sculpture

One week Carol Anne brought a box of wrapped objects, and Bobbi and she held a small-group discussion with five children about whether each item could be sculpture or not. There was consensus that a sculpture "has to be hard." The children didn't consider a cloth otter to be sculpture, for instance, because it was soft. They clarified that sculpture might be soft first and then harden, like clay. They became confused by a stone polar bear carving, struggling with whether something made of a natural material could only occur in nature. Scott, for example, decided, "It's not sculpture because it's made of rock." Interestingly, the children referred to molding with playdough or natural clay as *carving*—as in "carved out of playdough" . . . "carved out of clay." The discussion astonished us because it lasted over an hour, long and intense. Did the children understand that sculpture is something that is human-made? They were confused by items they interpreted to be rock. At one point, when asked if an object was sculpture, Nicolas said, "I don't know. It's very mysterious."

Some of the 4-year-olds showed a clear sense of aesthetic evaluation of objects. Ike, for example, considering a two-inch-high fuzzy teddy bear sitting on a miniature wooden chair, decided no, it wasn't a sculpture "because it doesn't look beautiful." He said this with gentleness, even tenderness, as if it were a great sorrow for the bear not to be sculpture.

Walks in the Community Challenge the Children's Concepts

Matthew, who loves to do things outdoors with the children, thought it would be interesting to go on a sculpture walk to see whether they could find any sculpture in the neighborhood. In March they went on several walks, photographing and investigating objects the children claimed were sculpture. Sometimes there were disagreements, such as one about a boulder inlaid with a bronze plaque:

"It's not sculpture. It's a rock."

"Yes, but it's got writing on it."

One boy insisted that the clamshell carrier for skis on the roof of a car was sculpture, but couldn't say why he thought so. The carrier was indeed a streamlined shape easily described as sculpturesque. We found this presence of aesthetic sense in 4-year-olds notable.

Matthew organized the photographs from the sculpture walks on three panels, set low to encourage interaction among the children and parents, and much discussion occurred as the children revisited them. Many other activities were taking place in the classroom simultaneously, such as a study of faces led by Annette, an interest in building that moved from blocks on the carpet to miniatures with toothpicks and modeling clay, as well as frequent play in housekeeping and story exploration in the library.

On another walk with Matthew, to a park bordering the ocean, the small group of children discovered an old military battery, with concrete steps, platforms, and two strange iron structures like huge bolts with a hinge on one side and a latch on the other:

"It's a sculpture! It's hard."

"It's not a sculpture."

"No, it's broken." [referring to the objects being rusty]

"No, because it opens and closes."

Here the children appeared to differentiate between objects that are practical and objects that are merely decorative. The concern for what is and what is not sculpture had captured the interest of most of the children in the classroom, and there was an implicit theory among them that if something had a practical function, then it was not sculpture.

Meanwhile, the classroom was flooded with images and discussion. Annette shared art books with sculptures by Michelangelo and others.

The Defining Characteristics

By late March, we could summarize the children's overall notions of sculpture as an object that (1) is made of hard material, (2) has no functional purpose, and (3) is visible and permanently saved for others to see. Some children thought sculpture should be beautiful, too. And there still was confusion over whether naturally occurring shapes, such as rocks, were sculpture, and over how sculpture is made.

Further Explorations in Making Sculpture

In late April, Tobias, age 4, brought in an object he described as "sculpture" from home and asked to have a small group with whom to share it. Five other boys were interested and formed a group, with Bobbi and Carol Anne, to discuss his pair of cast and painted plaster fighting dragons, wings wide and mouths stretched open in aggression.

Bobbi and Carol Anne later realized that a new understanding was occurring for the boys during their discussion:

"But how did they make the eye good?"

"Maybe it's glass."

"Because they are artists."

"Maybe they cooked it." [perhaps meaning fired in a kiln]

"Maybe they put it in the oven to dry up."

"It's not hot."

"Maybe they put it outside to cool."

"I was thinking about that."

When we reviewed the transcript of this conversation, we recognized how carefully the boys were thinking of "artists" in the process of making the dragons, hypothesizing intensely what might have happened to produce the sculpture, which had clear power for them.

Reflecting on their conversation, we better understood Nicolas's remark, "Maybe we should make the same thing!" This idea was immediately taken up by the group, spreading as quickly as wildfire, and propelled everyone to the studio area, where Bobbi handed out chunks of modeling clay. Much rolling of tails and pressing of bodies began. The boys worked furiously, with an urgency and concentration that had their teachers paying close attention and almost breathless. What Carol Anne calls the "windhorse effect" in emergent curriculum had happened. Borrowed from the secular Buddhist tradition of Shambhala (Trungpa 1987), the term refers to raising a "wind" of energy and alertness, a sense of being alive in the moment. Everyone could feel this energy all around the table, inside each of them—children and adults—a dynamic, positive, creative force.

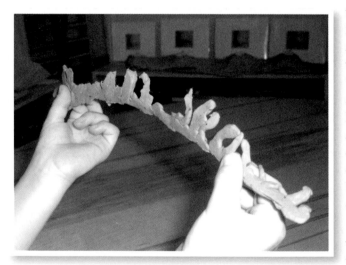

The boys made long flat bodies with spikes down the back and used tools to make eyes and stretching mouths. Knowing their interest in having their sculptures stand, Bobbi and Carol Anne commented that the sculpture Tobias had brought stood upright. "Ours are lying down," they countered. But shortly after, Tobias wanted his clay creation to stand, and Bobbi found a spatula so he could pry it off the table surface. Pointing to a shelf, she offered him a choice of bases—a rock or folded cardboard. Soon each boy chose a rock or cardboard base, attaching dragon bodies and long tails with spikes. The boys worked on their dragons without interruption for 80 minutes.

For days the boys did not touch their dragon work, sitting in view on a low table, but a week later they wanted to continue. We infer they needed an incubation period for their ideas to coalesce. On the next occasion they worked with equally furious concentration, several of them for over an hour. They added a base of black modeling clay "dirt," and made skulls like those they noticed on the base of the plaster dragon sculpture. They also wanted to add horns on their dragons. Another child commented, "Everyone is working fabulously!"

Nicolas had made a two-foot-long pencil-thin roll with spikes all along it—"the green dragon," he said. Together everyone studied the green dragon in the original sculpture, how its head and neck curved up into the air. Nicolas attempted to lift his figure, but it was too fragile and tore. Scott was having trouble making his horn stand up: It sagged.

Bobbi disappeared and quickly returned with wire and wire cutters. She demonstrated to Scott how to cut a length of wire as long as the horn he was working on. Together they folded the modeling clay around the wire and placed the horn on the dragon's head. Scott saw that it worked beautifully. Nicolas stopped his work to watch several children constructing horns and finally said, "I need wire." After cutting a two-foot piece, he began to push the wire into the thin strip of his dragon. The coordination required to push the wire into the thin roll was so delicate that the task was very difficult for Nicolas. After 10 minutes he was halfway; he wiped his forehead and went for a drink of water, fatigued by his intense effort.

We wondered whether he could continue. He returned, and took another 10 minutes to complete his self-set task. When finished, he immediately lifted the dragon into the air like a trophy. He was very pleased, as were we. We wondered whether Nicolas would think to bend the dragon's straight, pencil-thin body, but he didn't. The work of getting it up off the table and into the air was itself a triumph.

One boy worked with ease and dexterity in three dimensions, but the others struggled, motivated to make their dragons three-dimensional but terrifically challenged by the problem. Carol Anne speculates that they were trying to bring to modeling clay the "language" of their expectations for drawing (Malaguzzi in Gandini 2012; Steele 1998). The medium of clay demanded they learn a new "language"—new ways of moving their hands and of thinking, the properties of a new material, and the discipline necessary to master those properties and develop a new "literacy." Compared with drawing, mastery of clay requires the coordination of a third set of reference points: In addition to length and width, depth in space must be coordinated, requiring mathematical estimation.

Bobbi felt the task for her at this point was to support the children who were still working flat. What would help them understand the capacity of the material to work in three dimensions rather than two? What could she do so the young children could be comfortable with the material and create to their satisfaction?

Next Steps

In May, Bobbi and Annette brainstormed possible next steps in supporting the children's understanding of working in three dimensions. They decided to provide new materials and props for the children to explore—a wood plank base with three vertical rods, plus soft and bendable wire, netting, hardware cloth, and ribbons. The children could wind, bend, fold, and wrap these around the rods, exploring vertical space. The wrapping board opened up new interests in the classroom, creating a kind of playscape that drew in different children, including several girls.

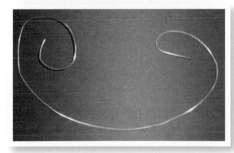

Nicolas enjoyed bending, folding, and wrapping the wire with an exploratory freedom. Suddenly it was more than a tool to allow his dragon to lift off the table. He cut a length of wire, coiled one end into a spiral, turned up the other end slightly, and declared, "I think I'm making a chameleon. See, this is its tail. Isn't it fabulous!" His wire de-

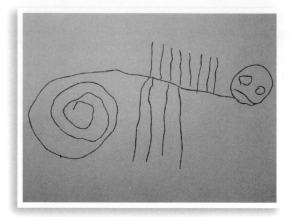

sign was precise, succinct, expressed, as wire suggests, in two dimensions. He commented that he didn't remember "what a chameleon looks like" and asked for a reference book: "I need to look in that book to make my sculpture." He studied the photos of a chameleon and asked to do a sketch to "remember what it looks like." After several sketches he produced one he was pleased with.

We could see so much potential in these actions. Would Nicolas grasp that he could use the wire frame as an armature for a clay sculpture? Would he prefer to keep wire as his sculpture medium? In addition, his capacity to generate ideas and to follow through in developing them was impressive. We saw that he had a sense of the preparatory work necessary for successful design because he wanted to modify his original wire artifact through studying a photo of a chameleon and sketching it before continuing.

But what happened next was one of those quirky, unexpected things that has no clear explanation except that it was unlikely it would have happened without everything that had occurred previously. It also shows how difficult it is to create nice, neat endings in a chapter like this. Here's what happened.

One day in June, Nicolas and Scott together decided to make an encyclopedia. Its illustrations would show all the different penguins they had found in learning how to review content in reference books. This activity began during a noon hour and lasted several days, and the work went from tight, restricted representations to a fluid expressivity that continues to astound us: How did Nicolas and Scott move from their previous level of drawing to this higher level of perceptual acuity and capacity to convey it? Who could have predicted that months of sculpture work would lead to fluent, graceful drawings?

Reflections

When a teacher sees a problem "as a direction," as Bobbi does, reflection becomes closely linked to planning the next step. Planning that is closely linked to a specific challenge, such as how to help children work in three dimensions, is suspenseful and uncertain, because teachers do not know how the events will work out. Everyone gets excited to see what will happen.

The Value of Documentation

Documentation helps teachers study what children understand and to plan what to do: We find it a crucial aid to reflection on teaching and learning. At Peter Green Hall, teachers use documentation as a habit of teaching. They alter displays weekly, providing a focus for conversation among children, teachers, families, and visitors. The development of these pedagogical skills has been part of the influence on the center of the Reggio Emilia experience (Cadwell 2003; Edwards, Gandini, & Forman 2012; Wien 2008). Without such documentation, the teachers might never have seen the children's initial frustration with playdough in a busy classroom.

In early June, we studied the documentation generated since January (36 pages of notes and transcripts, 100–120 digital images printed for individual portfolios and classroom documentation). It was only after we had reviewed the documentation from January to May, discussing what was most significant in terms of challenges to the children and tracing their development in those challenges as well as the teacher responses to those problems, that we saw clearly that Nicolas had shifted from using a straight wire in his dragon to working with wire with ease and facility to make a chameleon. Without the review of the documentation, we would not have seen the arc of development in his use of materials.

Teacher Decision Making

How do teachers decide what to plan, what resources to have available, and what to offer as supportive scaffolding when engaging in emergent curriculum? We found in this case that the intriguing nature of the overall question—*What do young children think sculpture is?*—gave us direction. Our own sense of inquiry into what children think suggested possibilities for what to ask or try. Such inquiry engages us in problem solving. And a move that does not work well is seen not as an error but rather as a step toward what will work: Teaching is self-correcting.

Children Learning, Teachers Learning

Throughout this project, the children understood that their ideas mattered and that they could participate in deciding what to do—such as offering a sculpture for discussion and deciding to re-create it. They understood they could trust teachers with their ideas, and that teachers would support their intentions—such as compiling a penguin encyclopedia. These are powerful learnings for children in a democracy; they will help the children learn how to participate in group decision making.

The teachers learned much about letting children explore and plan in an area they themselves scarcely knew about. We had no idea of the potential of sculpture for children this age. The fact that the children thought of their work as sculpture deepened their levels of exploration and conceptualization: It made their efforts more serious. The teachers learned as much as the children, and this joining of minds enlivens teaching and makes every move fresh and stimulating. The joy of a project is in its continual surprises and in the capacity of everyone involved to participate in this joy. The work was disciplined and focused, and it built skill in both children and teachers from week to week.

It is the capacity of emergent curriculum to create joy that makes it memorable, sustainable, and unmatched in developing identity, culture, and attachment in both children and their teachers.

Carol Copple

"Your Ideas Are Important"

Carol Anne Wien's work always inspires me. She is a highly lucid, engaging writer and a thoughtful student of teaching and learning. Perhaps most importantly, she does much of her work in the midst of classroom activity and teachers' planning sessions, listening attentively to the teachers and children. In "Moving Into Uncertainty: Sculpture With 3- to 5-Year-Olds," we see the abundant fruits of Carol Anne's in-the-thick-of-it approach to understanding teaching and learning.

Carol Anne and her coauthors take us to Peter Green Hall, the Halifax, Nova Scotia, center where Bobbi-Lynn Keating, Annette Coates Comeau, and Barbara Bigelow work. The center serves a group of children that is diverse both culturally and economically. Inspired by the Reggio Emilia experience, the teachers there support the children in developing their ideas with, as Carol Anne puts it, "strong purposeful curriculum activities embedded with rich learning." Following the direction of children's interests and thinking in a sustained, reflective way is what gives the Reggio experience such rich results. It is not a matter of simply harvesting all themes or projects from what the children do and say spontaneously. Instead, it is what teachers do with a given topic or project that matters most. Teachers help children deepen their thinking through an extended, in-depth focus on a topic or investigation and the careful thought they give to what they might provide, comment on, or ask children.

In Reggio-inspired programs like this one, teachers are always selecting from the many things children say or do—those ideas and topics that seem to reveal promising openings for further investigation. Often a comment or action conveys something the teachers did not realize about a child's thought or interest, as with Omar's assertion "It's not playdough. It's sculpture." This was the starting point for the investigation that develops.

What do the teachers do next? They make sculpting materials available and explore children's ideas about sculpture. They continually reflect together about what is happening in the classroom. They carefully observe and document the children's actions and questions at every stage, and use these observations to guide their efforts to provoke further thought and creation. The teachers always want to see how far children can take an idea on their own, but they are also aware that at times they can help move things forward by a "provocation" or by "loaning their knowledge" (Malaguzzi 1998). For example, when the children are wrestling with the problem of how to make their sculptures stand up, Annette shows them possibilities with wire.

There is more than one important consequence of the Reggio experience of building curriculum on children's ideas and documenting their work. Besides ensuring that the resulting projects are of interest to the children, this kind of learning experience makes a very potent point to them: *Your ideas are important.* The power of this message cannot be overstated. When children know that adults value their ideas, they take their own thinking and efforts seriously. They put themselves fully into solving a problem or making an idea work. They listen to each other to get information and ideas. They are truly a community of learners.

Evident in this chapter are a number of take-away lessons, whether or not teachers work in a Reggio-inspired or other emergent curriculum program. Among these lessons, here are some that seem particularly valuable to me.

- **It is important to attend to children's ideas and give them weight in the life of the classroom.** How teachers respond to what children say is always significant. It doesn't always take the form of launching a project or study. It is also in practices like writing children's ideas on a flip chart, respectfully displaying their work, asking questions that follow up on what they say, and showing excitement when children do or say things that are clearly important to them.

- **There is great value in providing time and opportunity for children to dig into a topic or investigation over a sustained period.** Too often in early childhood programs, the curriculum skips around, doing a holiday activity here and a field trip there, without the kind of long-term, in-depth focus that results in greater understanding and stronger interest. With extended periods of time and sustained investigation, children are able to develop more meaningful connections and construct ideas of greater complexity.

- **It is important for teachers to reflect on their own and with others (and at times with families) about how the children's ideas are developing and how they can be expanded and deepened.** As Tiziana Filippini (1990) said, using a favorite Reggio metaphor: "We must be able to catch the ball that the children throw us, and toss it back to them in a way that makes the children want to continue the game with us, developing, perhaps, other games as we go along." At each juncture, thoughtful consideration of how to "toss the ball back" to provoke children's thinking is a critical part of teachers' reflection and planning together.

Carol Anne's ongoing work with the Halifax center and this particular chapter—children exploring and creating sculpture—offer much to inspire us all.

....

Carol Copple, PhD, is an educational consultant living in Nashville, Tennessee. For 17 years she headed the NAEYC publications program, authored numerous books, and played a leading role in developing the Association's position statements and education initiatives.

PART THREE

Difficult Life Events as Curriculum

Chapter 8

**Carol Anne Wien,
Bobbi-Lynn Keating,
Justin West, and
Barbara Bigelow**

A Mommy Breast and a Daddy Breast: Encountering Illness as Emergent Curriculum

A visitor to Peter Green Hall Children's Centre's classroom for 4- and 5-year-olds broke down in tears when she saw their teacher Bobbi-Lynn Keating with a head bald from chemotherapy. The visitor said her sister-in-law had recently died of breast cancer. In the family's desperate need to cope with the situation, their children, 4 and 6 years old, were not involved in the process. Now one was very angry.

Adults in distress, racing to cope with unbearable difficulty, may be forgiven much. We tell the following story about the way children and adults in one classroom encountered and experienced a teacher's cancer to share the sense of a community of care and the emotional depth that resulted. Such stories overturn stereotypes about what preschool-age children can handle.

The question of how to handle difficult news raises issues for early childhood educators. There may be as many ways to face crises as there are people facing them. We accept that the person with the diagnosis of cancer has some right to determine how it is experienced and, through our Reggio-inspired practice, that children have rights of participation. What follows seemed to be the right approach in this context, for this event, and for the children, families, and teachers involved.

After 13 years of transformation, Peter Green Hall has expanded from developmentally appropriate practice to emergent and Reggio-inspired early childhood practices with highly participatory structures and continuous collaboration among children, families, and teachers. The classroom environments and garden have evolved to build connections both to children's and teachers' interests and to the local community. The center supports children, teachers, and families in believing in their ideas and in their participation to realize those ideas in daily life. This sensibility promotes both democratic citizenship and the satisfaction of contributing in a productive way to collective life and happiness. How is this mission sustained when a teacher is diagnosed with cancer? What happens when a difficult issue is welcomed in a classroom for young children?

Illness Discovered

When Bobbi, at 37, was diagnosed with invasive ductal carcinoma, she said:

> "I was propelled into a club of pink ribbons I wanted no part of. I was flooded with emotions—shock, fear, sadness, resentment, anger. When I thought of the children I work with, I thought surely they would notice my breast gone, my hair loss. What would I tell them? In the midst of my panic, I had a moment of clarity. Why would I treat this topic as any different from anything else? We dealt with difficult topics before—a knee surgery, and the death of a family pet. I believe children are capable, ready to engage, to learn. Gandini's quote on the image of children is one I hold on to:
>
>> All children have preparedness, potential, curiosity, and interest in constructing their learning; in engaging in social interactions and negotiating everything that the environment brings them. (Gandini 1993, 5)
>
> "If you believe this, it's a no-brainer that a teacher's experience with cancer is a topic that would be discussed, documented, researched, and experienced in the classroom."

The Center Responds

The center staff gathered together to discuss the situation and what to do, right after Bobbi's diagnosis. The range of responses was as wide as we would expect, with artist and associate director, Annette Coates, articulating many of our conventional reactions—What will the parents think? Won't it be too difficult for the children? How will we contain our own emotions if we share the news? Bobbi spoke up about her own need to keep her integrity and credibility with the children through honest communication. Many staff said they would support whatever Bobbi wished to do—to support her wishes was the strongest response they could offer. Her coteachers Justin West and Angela Silva agreed. Before talking about the situation with the children, the staff and director discussed with the families how they would share the news with the children. The parents knew the center well after several years of participation, and they supported the decision to involve the children. The director, Barbara Bigelow, said, "There was so much trust from parents, not one negative comment."

This chapter was first published in the March 2012 issue of *Young Children.*

The Children Respond

Before Bobbi met with the children, she made a conscious decision not to use the powerful word *cancer*. She spoke with the children about having some diseased tissue—a lump in her breast, which had to be removed by surgery. She talked briefly about "chemo" as medicine she would need. Bobbi reported that "the children wanted to see the lump. Luckily, removing my shirt and showing my tank top with two obvious breasts was satisfactory." When she asked the children if they understood what was happening, they made comments such as,

> "Your breast will be flat."
>
> "You'll only have one breast, right?"
>
> "You'll have a mommy breast and a daddy breast."

In the next days, the children asked questions and shared their thoughts:

> "Is your lump still there?"
>
> "Can you grow a new breast?"
>
> "No, you'll have to buy one," said one boy.

As part of the morning program each day, the center organizes small groups. Each teacher has a group of children for an extended time focused on a specific area of classroom interest. Each child chooses which group they wish to join. Bobbi's group gave the children opportunities to discuss this issue further, and their comments offered interesting glimpses into the children's thinking.

Their thoughts ranged from the practicalities of how the lump would be removed, as in "They will cut it and make a circle and take out the tissue" and "The doctor will look in there with a flashlight," to larger questions of sexual identity, as in

> "Do I have a breast?" asked Barry.
>
> "No," said Dylan, "boys don't have breasts 'cause boys don't have babies."
>
> "You'll have a flat one—one big, one flat."
>
> "Yeah, a flat one like a boy."
>
> "But I think you will still be a girl."

The teachers documented children's thoughts and images and shared them with parents, who organized their own email conference to offer support and communication. Parents of children formerly at the center contacted the center again when they heard the news, and other classrooms were also involved. There is no question we were all grief stricken, yet the children's responses helped ground us.

After Surgery

When Bobbi returned to work following surgery, the children wanted to confirm their understanding, and asked, "Is your lump gone? Is your breast gone now?" And they wanted to see, to know for sure. Bobbi was prepared for this, and revealed her tank top, one side clearly flat. The children then asked to see her flat breast. She showed them the scar,

which relieved the children, because they related it to their own cuts and Band-Aid stories. We found it interesting that in their drawings, showing Bobbi with one breast, they always drew her smiling.

Facing six rounds of chemotherapy between December and April, Bobbi prepared the children for the fact she would lose her hair. Parents brought in wigs and hats that became playful objects for everyone.

The children also noticed around this time that Bobbi had two breasts again, and wondered whether her breast grew back. She showed them her foam prosthesis. The children called it a "toy breast" and found it of great interest. They passed it around, and both girls and boys tried it under their own shirts. When they arrived in the morning, they often asked for it. The prosthesis became part of classroom life, requested and passed around from child to child like a transitional object—something that reminds one of strong emotional connection (Winnicott 2005). By sharing this object, the children felt closer to Bobbi, and we think that it helped make the disease seem smaller and more manageable. At the same time, the children's matter-of-fact response and engagement lifted the adults' spirits.

During Treatment

On December 24, Bobbi was hospitalized because of low blood counts and a fever. Her hair fell out. To prepare the children for her hair loss, Justin and Matthew photographed themselves with her when they visited her at the hospital, and brought the photo into the classroom. The children did not recognize Bobbi in the photo, asking Justin,

"Is that your family?"

"It's David in the middle. No, it's Bobbi."

"She looks like a monkey."

"Is she still a girl, or is she a boy?"

"She is a girl, but she looks like a monkey because her hair is short on her head."

The children's empathy was fully engaged when they heard Bobbi spent Christmas in the hospital. They were incredulous that "she didn't have a Christmas tree!" They had a hard time believing that such a thing could happen, and planned to create a tree with presents for her when she returned to the center. It was at this point that a different level of concern for Bobbi's illness emerged. Perry asked, "Is Bobbi going to come back?" When Justin explained she had to be healthy enough to return, one child explained,

"Because she has no antibodies."

"What are antibodies?" someone asked.

"That's something you can't see, only if you look through a microscope. It fights germs in your body," Dylan explained.

The fact that a 5-year-old could define antibodies with clarity reminds us of the power of children's intelligence.

In January, for the first time since the saga began in September, the children used the word cancer. They asked,

"What is cancer?"

"Why does Bobbi have it?"

"How did she get it?"

"Where *is* Bobbi?"

These questions arose in a large-group conversation when Bobbi was absent. Justin reported that the questions were so difficult—for adults as well as for the children—that when an interruption occurred he let the questions go, wanting to respond but not knowing what to say. There is no doubt that this was a courageous project for us to tackle, because the uncertainties and adult limitations in controlling our own emotions were so abundantly clear throughout. From December through April, Bobbi worked most days, with a few days off following each chemo treatment every third week. During this time, the other adults in the classroom, Justin and Angela, carried a heavy load, more aware than others of how ill Bobbi was, and struggling to hold the program together for the children and families.

Bobbi Returns to the Classroom

When Bobbi first returned to work in January, Justin brought in a tree and the children decorated it with ornaments and pink ribbons. Someone made a cake, and the children made cards and gifts and wore pink clothes to give Bobbi the Christmas she had missed. Bobbi, while still finding "the pink ribbon stuff" annoying, also found her revulsion toward it had subsided. Carol Anne Wien thought that wearing pink clothes allowed the children to take action in a way that spoke to their attachment to Bobbi and their empathy for her. Pink items became additional transitional objects creating a bond among the group, and the party celebrated Bobbi's return.

The greatest difficulty for the children, as for many adults, was the change in Bobbi's appearance. Without hair, pale and gaunt, she was noticeably ill, though still able to work with focus and energy when present. It is at this point that many cancer patients suffer the indignity of the loss of personal identity and visibly take on the identity of "cancer patient." As the children said,

"You had the chemo and that made your hair fall out."

"You're still Bobbi, though, right?"

To keep working meant that she could still be Bobbi, keeping her professional identity intact.

Bobbi's bald head provoked some interesting negotiation between her and the children. She did not want to wear a wig or a hat—it was too unlike her. She did try wearing a hat for several days, but kept taking it off, which bothered the children. She offered a small-group meeting to discuss the situation, and the children said:

"You don't look like you."

"There's black things on your head [stubble]. It scares me."

Doreen drew Bobbi with stubble and other children drew her with hair. "I gave you hair, Bobbi, so you would look pretty."

The children also spontaneously began to try to make hair for Bobbi, using large pleated coffee filters as caps, and taping strips of paper to the edges. When presented with one of these, Bobbi refused to wear it. Carol Anne thought this moment was the location of a significant emotional tension or "knot." The children's need to restore Bobbi to the way they previously knew her met Bobbi's need to be accepted as she was in her illness—to be visible rather than to hide the illness. She refused to wear the paper construction, saying, "I look like death warmed over already. I'm not wearing that." For Bobbi, it was a question of dignity. Perhaps it illustrates the point that the cancer patient is bearing the illness and cannot also be asked to take on the burden of other people's distress about the situation. When compelling needs of children and adults intersect, it reminds us that the needs and rights of both must always be negotiated and balanced.

One day Bobbi tried out a headscarf as a new solution to this dilemma. This sparked a desire among the children to wear headscarves too, and Justin and Angela tore up fabric to make little scarves for the children. Most people in the classroom wore them for several days. Then a child said, "I don't want it anymore," and Bobbi replied, "Me neither." From then on her bald head was accepted.

Bobbi's final treatment was in early April. In mid-May, she was well enough to travel to Ottawa, the capital of Canada, where she was one of 10 national recipients of the Prime Minister's Award for Excellence in Early Childhood Education. The recipients came from across Canada and attended a weeklong program of events in recognition of the high quality of their contributions to their professional field, both in their work settings and in leadership roles in their communities. Bobbi did not receive the award because she had cancer—her nomination letter referred to previous work—but the way she and the center handled her cancer experience was indicative of the way they approach the experience of life lived, in all things, with children. The award provided a strong affirmation of this approach.

The Power of Emergent Curriculum

Reflections

We have many thoughts on creating curriculum from a difficult issue and suggest but several of these in our reflections.

Our Own Limits

The teachers documented the narrative of events and the children's comments, questions, and drawings, and made them available on the documentation shelf for parents and children at arrival and departure. One visitor saw the documentation and asked, "Who would do a project on cancer? Isn't this self-serving?" This individual understood the work much better after attending a local conference presentation where the teachers shared this narrative and its documentation.

While we do not know the interpretation the visitor gave to "self-serving," we would agree that it was—in the sense of giving visibility and credibility to a teacher's personal situation that was unbearably difficult, even for a community prepared to offer its care. Yet the diagnosis of breast cancer is so common among women, and some men, that it showed the children one possible way this trauma could be lived through with others. There is no question the children will meet it again in their future, given its presence as an aspect of our lives. Who among us has not lost someone to breast cancer?

We recognize that there were times when the difficulty of the situation left the other teachers in the room unable to respond. When children asked, "Is Bobbi coming back?" this was also the adults' question. Would she make it through a treatment that was making her so sick? Justin said that the children's questions— What is cancer? Why did Bobbi get it?— were exactly the same as the adults' questions. The adults had no answers. They held themselves together for the children, focusing on the program and concentrating on not breaking down. While there were many other curriculum topics of ongoing interest during this time, such as creating a swamp for the classroom, a six-month project to create a restaurant, and a project to collect pennies for a school in Africa, Bobbi's cancer, as Barb said, "would break through other curriculum like a wound."

A question concerning cancer as emergent curriculum with young children is whether it asks too much of staff, children, and families, as Annette initially wondered. For example, one child in the after-school program said she thought this was what her school principal had. She was right, but the elementary school children had not been told. Does it protect children to keep them apart from it? Or does it isolate and remove children's power to act? We want to reiterate that there are likely as many ways of approaching crises of illness as there are people facing them, and those involved in each case need the freedom to seek out the best way of coping.

Reflections on Encountering Illness as Emergent Curriculum

There are many approaches to supporting teachers through illness. The following are the aspects we found most helpful:

- Include children and families, and share what happens.

- Talk candidly, using accurate language for what happens.

- Use documentation to make the situation visible and to allow children and adults to talk about it openly. It helps people feel more comfortable.

- Listen to the children, observe their actions, and respond to their initiatives.

- Prepare children for changes, such as Justin's sharing the photo of Bobbi without hair.

- Answer children's questions simply but honestly.

- Respect the sick person's needs, as for example, when Bobbi did not want to wear the paper hair the children made for her.

Director Barb said, "You could feel the weight of the situation through the whole center." Parents would ask staff how Bobbi was doing, staff would offer a palatable summary, then some parents would cry and leave. This left staff with an unresolved emotional burden. While Bobbi had the release of the direct work with the children, other staff had no such release from the burden of care, worry, and love for Bobbi. In retrospect, Barb says, "We should have had some support for the staff." Justin, for example, had to carry the program in the classroom for 4- and 5-year-olds and help mentor Bobbi's student teacher when Justin himself was still a fairly new teacher. Justin and Angela also witnessed ways Bobbi was ill that she managed to cover from others in the center. We acknowledge these burdens because we do not wish to downplay the challenges or consequences of sharing the provocation of a cancer diagnosis with children and families.

On the other hand, this burden of illness and care for Bobbi brought the community of parents, children, and staff together in a close shared bond as they worked to meet the challenge. Because of limited sick leave provisions in child care, the parents raised funds for Bobbi and the center. And for Bobbi, there was no question that "the children got me through it."

Empathy: The Most Significant Consequence

Goleman describes how feelings are "the bedrock of communication" and how neuroscience has found mirror neurons in humans, which means that emotion in one human is easily mirrored or produced in another—seeing someone hurt also hurts us and we respond (Goleman 2006, 37, 57). Kagan believes empathy is an ethical sense built in by biology:

> Although humans inherit a biological bias that permits them to feel anger, jealousy, selfishness, and envy, and to be rude, aggressive, or violent, they inherit an even stronger biological basis for kindness, compassion, cooperation, love, and nurture—especially toward those in need. (Goleman 2006, 62)

Bobbi was touched by the children's desire to make her gifts—the missed Christmas tree in January, the gift of hair in drawings and coffee filter caps, and spontaneous food treats when they knew she needed special food. The impulse to offer a gift is one of the ways humans attempt to care for others in difficult situations and is clearly present in young children. Perhaps the strangest gift of all was the ritual that developed around Bobbi's departure every three weeks for chemotherapy. The children gathered at the window overlooking the spot where her husband picked her up, insisted the window be open, and watched her go, waving and calling out, "Have a good chemo! Have a good chemo!"

For the adults, "have a good chemo" could be nothing but ironic, given how sick it made Bobbi and how she hated going for it. How could such a harrowing experience be good? Yet, a good chemo would surely "get" the cancer, so it made sense too. For the children, it seemed to be a simple marker to acknowledge the situation as best they could, and their cheerfulness gave others a lift.

Bobbi's assessment of this work with children as an emergent curriculum was that the project did not have conceptual depth in which much new knowledge was

Children's Books About Cancer

Moore-Mallinos, J. 2008. *Mom Has Cancer!* Hauppauge, NY: Barron's Educational Series.

Sachedina, S. 2005. *Metu and Lee Learn About Breast Cancer*. Winter Park, FL: Dr. Shenin Sachedina Medical Educational Products. www.metuandlee.com

Sutherland, E. 2007. *Mom and the Polka-Dot Boo-Boo: A Gentle Story Explaining Breast Cancer to a Young Child*. Atlanta, GA: American Cancer Society.

Theis, P., & M. Theis. 2008. *Clarabelle the Cat Loses Her Hair*. Indianapolis, IN: Dog Ear Publishing.

produced or enjoyed; rather it had emotional depth and gravity. Center staff commented on how empathetic the children who shared that experience became. Angela said, "It was pretty hard because Bobbi was so sick. It made me realize how empathetic the children are—they really cared." In Bobbi's view, the children's empathy goes beyond any she has seen in her 20-year career: "Those children are kinder, gentler, they have so much more empathy; It was empowering for them."

How were the children empowered? They were able to comment, to ask questions, to draw their responses, to share their fears, to create events such as a January Christmas party or rituals such as "Have a good chemo," and to make things such as paper hair. They were able to offer their gifts, and in so doing, participate fully in the relationship created out of the difficult context.

When people we love face difficulty, all we can do is take small actions that might make things better for them, and for their caregivers, and surround them with our care and support as a community attuned to hurt and the need to assuage it. That these children had such gifts to offer to Bobbi and to the community of the center speaks to the quality of their social and emotional intelligence and their freedom to participate. As Bobbi said, "It was the children who got me through it." It is not that adults would ask children to do so, but that their empathy and care contributed in an essential way to the healing of others. We are happy to report that at this time, several years later, Bobbi is healthy and working full-time, and those children and their parents still visit frequently.

Susan Fraser

When Everyday Life Is the Curriculum

Over the years it has been my visits to early childhood settings like Peter Green Hall Children's Centre in Halifax that have given me hope that we can achieve high-quality child care in North America inspired by the municipal preschools in Reggio Emilia, Italy. I was introduced to Peter Green Hall by Carol Anne Wien after I had returned from a visit to Reggio Emilia in 1993. Since then I have visited the program several times. In June 2006, I participated in a master class in emergent curriculum. Barbara Bigelow, the program director, wrote in the introduction to the class, "The staff at Peter Green Hall since 1996 have been influenced by the ideas and practices of the Reggio Emilia approach but have not copied them. Rather they take Reggio ideas and practices as points of departure for rethinking their own practices." I have seen over time that although their program reflected many of the principles of the Reggio Emilia experience, they had developed their own unique philosophy and practices. They have created an environment and program that reflects their own values and context on the east coast of Canada.

The last time I visited the center was in 2011 when my granddaughter Alison was a student at Dalhousie University and her two children were enrolled in the child care center. She told me that she would never have made it through law school without the support of the center and the circle of relationships that surround it. As I read the chapter about Bobbi-Lynn Keating's experience of sharing her illness with the children, teachers, and their families in her classroom, and thinking of Alison and her children's experiences in the center, I was even more aware of how the foundational principles of Reggio Emilia—such as relationship, respect, reciprocity, and transparency—have inspired this program. It is evident in all the center does that teachers view children as strong, competent, resourceful, and interested in constructing their own learning. As I read about how the teachers shared Bobbi's experience with cancer with the children, I could see how all these principles support the teachers in their decision to be open and honest with the children and their families about what Bobbi was going through. In fact, I thought, how could Bobbi *not* have shared her experience of going through chemotherapy with the children and their families when these principles are at the core of her work with children? Values such as truth, honesty, and trusting in children's abilities and parental support guide teachers' responses to Bobbi's illness. Furthermore, when I visited the center in April 2011, Bobbi told me, "We don't have big projects, it is everyday life (that interests us)."

Everyday life, however, is likely to bring up topics that can be very challenging. This was especially true when honest communication and integrity mean that staff could not hide Bobbi's cancer from the children. As described in this chapter, all through this example of emergent curriculum, adults handle difficult issues with sensitivity. The adults and children also show respect for Bobbi's feelings and what she was going through. One of the issues the children struggled with was Bobbi's change of identity: physically her loss of hair and body shape. One child said, "You are still Bobbi, right?"

The teachers think carefully about the language they use. They decide to avoid the word *cancer* and call it *diseased tissue*. They explain that *chemo* is the medicine Bobbi needs to get better. The children are able to use the vocabulary they learn to call out to her as she leaves to get her treatment, "Have a good chemo!" Helping children acquire the necessary vocabulary is one of the strategies that empowers children to talk openly about a difficult topic.

One of the biggest challenges is how to cope with people's feelings of distress and how these can surface unexpectedly. It is particularly hard for Bobbi, who is coping with her own emotions, to deal with other people's distress at her situation. Strategies for coping include providing ways for the children and parents to show their feelings in positive ways, such as bringing in wigs and hats the children can explore and use during dramatic play. Fellow teacher, Justin West, brings in a Christmas tree to decorate in January because the children are worried that Bobbi had been in hospital and missed Christmas. In this way everyone can show their concern and affection for Bobbi in supportive ways.

I see the thread of Reggio inspiration woven into all aspects of the program and in the materials adults provide for children to make their thinking visible. For instance, on one occasion children chose coffee filters and strips of paper to make hair. Another time the teachers offer pens and paper so children can draw portraits of how Bobbi looked as she lost her hair. I see the influence of Reggio Emilia in the documentation and in the shared information that happened naturally as small groups of children discussed difficult issues such as Bobbi's bald head: "Is she still a girl or is she a boy?" . . . "Can you grow a new breast?" . . . "Will Bobbi come back?" Teachers are able to listen to children, hear their concerns, and together discuss ideas for how to support Bobbi.

Children, families, and teachers sharing an experience as deeply moving as the one shared in this chapter recognize how helpful it is to be able to communicate feelings openly and honestly. Everyone benefits from being part of a supportive group. It must have given the parents and teachers an appreciation of children's strength. The children learn about honesty, resilience, and empathy—qualities that help prepare them for life as adults. As for Bobbi, readers can't help but think of how brave and courageous she is. The love and affection of everyone for Bobbi, I am sure, must have carried her through and helped her survive the ordeal.

....

Susan Fraser, MA, is a retired instructor in early childhood in New Westminster, British Columbia, Canada, and an author with a particular interest in the Reggio Emilia experience.

Chapter 9

**Carol Anne Wien,
Matthew Sampson,
Justin West, and
Barbara Bigelow**

Zombie World: Boys Invent a Culture in Their After-School Program

Five boys rush to gather materials—paper, pencils or fine-tipped markers, scissors, tape—as they arrive in the classroom of their after-school program. They seat themselves at a table near a huge sprawling pencil drawing hung on the wall nearby: It looks like a map of a city. They set to work drawing small figures whose torsos consist of a rectangle crossed with a large X. Two younger boys arrive, rush to the table, asking if today they can be "cutters." An older boy responds, "Today you can be tapers."

We choose to share the children's creation of their "Zombie World" for several reasons. The first is that it illustrates the quality of *emergence* in curriculum that occurs in a program where the children's ideas are embraced and supported. This quality of emergence has an energy that Carol Anne Wien calls the "windhorse effect" (Wien 2008, 159)—an uplifted positive energy that sweeps through the community as children wish to be part of a shared experience of making and doing. We believe we witnessed, in this project, a culture of childhood made visible through the children's activity and our documentation: We use the term *culture* here in a sense interpreted from Reggio educators, whereby children create their own perspective on aspects of their society (see Davoli & Ferri 2000; Gandini 2012). As we embraced possibilities, and supported the children, we allowed these possibilities to expand rather than confining them.

A second reason we share the story is the impact on us of deciding to share the project outside our program at Peter Green Hall Children's Centre. Teachers Matthew Sampson and Justin West returned from a study tour of the infant and toddler centers and preschools of Reggio Emilia, Italy, with a new understanding of possibilities for building relationships between children's activity in the center and the local community (see Delrio 2012; Piccinini & Giudici 2012). Their desire to expand relationships between the children in our center and places in our local community became a conscious goal for the program: How might those connections be cultivated? What forms could they take?

A third reason is to explore the meaning of the eruption of violent themes in the midst of the project—"violence" as the presence in the children's work of weapons of war (soldiers, guns, cannons, shooting, and so forth)—and to consider the teachers' intentional response to these depictions of violence (see Bergen 1994; Levin & Carlsson-Paige 2005). We wish to share Matthew's approach in particular, as a topic of discussion, something to question and reflect upon as we consider its implications for adult-child relationships (Marion 2011).

Yet another reason is that this project was the work (almost exclusively) of boys ages 3–8. Carol Anne wonders whether the fact that their teachers were male made a difference to the children, and whether this project would have occurred in the same way with female teachers. She wonders because of the startling gender difference in reaction to the project when the female teachers first heard about it. This project raised all sorts of interesting and difficult questions for us to consider.

The Activation of the Project

Matthew leads the after-school classroom, for 26 children (16 boys and 10 girls during this particular year) from 5 to 10 years of age. They attend the center before school, during lunch hour, and after school, walked between center and school by their teachers. The Zombie World project began in January 2011 as an ordinary moment that arose out of a problem for two boys in the after-school classroom.

Pete and Todd, two older boys, complained to Matthew on the walk from school to the center about a homework assignment for which they had to create a newscast report, "and that would be so boring." But Matthew responded with a different view:

> Matthew: "Maybe you could make it fun, report on something fake and exciting!"
>
> Boys: "Like what?"
>
> Matthew: "Like a news video. Say there is a huge storm coming and you are in Hawaii."

Matthew's *provocation*—that, in contrast to their flat affect, the assignment could be fun and exciting—stimulated the boys once back in the after-school program to create characters for their newscast in pencil drawings.

As they drew, the two boys were flooded with ideas for characters and settings and decided to create a "post-apocalyptic zombie newscast" in comic book form. The next day they continued drawing, with Todd creating first a spaceship then a submarine for his character. The third day the boys taped their two drawings together to create a connected set of images. Two other boys began to work with them, creating characters and additional "rooms" for the submarine. Each addition was the living space for an individual character, imaginatively connected to the submarine by tubes and doorways, and literally connected with tape to the original drawing.

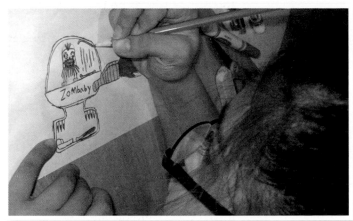

Matthew reports that he recognized when Pete and Todd taped their drawings together that something bigger than a homework assignment was about to happen: The invention of characters Zomboy and Zombaby and their submarine had taken on a life of its own. The homework assignment was completed for its due date and disappeared behind the excitement of the boys' joint creation of characters and settings. For the next two weeks, five of the boys in the after-school group continued drawing characters and rooms in pencil on paper, taping each addition to the original drawings. At this point, the construction became too large for any table in the room and was moved to the block area, where it could "live" and grow day by day. As the drawing continued into the third week, there emerged, or settled down, a schema for representing a "zombie"—its essential feature, an X on a rectangle.

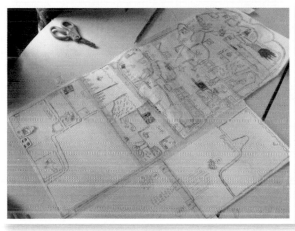

More children joined the drawing, including one younger sister, who created a room of pink hearts and furniture for a Zombie Queen. She remained the sole girl to participate, although she did so only for a short period of time. A hierarchy organized by the participants also emerged. Matthew says, "Because Todd and Pete had started the drawing, they were first and second boss." Next in the hierarchy were those joining the drawing of zombies or "making money." Below these in the hierarchy were the "cutters" and "tapers," roles the older boys found for younger children wanting to participate. The boys began to call their paper construction "Zombie World."

As the drawing grew bigger and bigger, each additional room like the cells of a growing organism, the children also self-organized a means of mass-producing zombies. They organized an assembly line of drawers and cutters and tapers, in their (age-related) hierarchy of dominance, producing sheets of little cutout figures that could, with a piece of tape on the back, be moved about from one part of the map of their "world" to another. A month after it began, the drawing was so large it was hung on a wall. The boys involved were obsessed with it, rushing in after school each day to draw their imagined characters, events, and settings.

Here Comes Violence

About four weeks into their drawing efforts, the boys began to mass-produce a zombie army. They prepared sheets of the zombie figures using their rectangle crossed with X schema and made small changes for different roles. One child would draw the basic zombie schema, for instance, then pass it on to another to make the lines for rifles. Someone else would create trucks, tanks, jets—and a huge army of parachuting turtles. Next came drawings of monsters, guns accompanied by explicit sound effects—*rat-a-tat-tat*—as they were drawn, an all-out war with guns shooting and bombs falling. Grenades, bombs, machine guns, cannons, and sharks that spewed money, zombie pizza chefs, and the "Uncle Sam" icon conflated with a zombie schema to draft volunteers for their army. The reach of the "Uncle Sam" figure into distant areas in Canada, and into the minds of 8-year-olds, astonished us.

How did the teachers approach the children's representation of violence? The answer begins several years earlier, when Matthew discovered that Todd had drawn figures being stabbed, and Matthew had asked Todd to talk about it. When Todd's response was, "I don't know," Matthew had said to him, "If you're not going to talk about it, then don't draw it in my classroom." In this earlier response we see a pattern common among many early childhood educators, of shutting down a child's involvement in an activity of which the adult disapproves (Bergen 1994). Perhaps the activity frightens us too much, or we worry where it will lead. Will children become violent by representing violence? Does the adult give permission to be violent by allowing such activity to continue?

This time, however, Matthew did not shut down the children's activity. The violence was symbolic and fully contained in the world of drawings the children were creating. In drawing, the children had contained violence in a safe place where they had control over it (Paley 2005). But what if the representations did spill over into real violence among the children? This time, because the children's excitement was so contagious and their impulse to create so cooperative, the teachers saw, contrary to the topic itself, not conflict but the building of community, as others have also seen in similar contexts (Detour & Logue 2011).

For Matthew, not halting the depiction of war and violence was a change in his teaching practice. He described to Carol Anne how not shutting down the representation of violence was both a way of valuing the intense imaginative activity that so engaged the children and a way of respecting the thoughts and feelings of the children. He saw his more recent response as a change for the better in his teaching practice.

Still, the violence theme was worrisome for him: "We thought it might be going too far, but we did not interfere or

The Power of Emergent Curriculum

censor the work." How might it be going too far? For Matthew, his worry was not about the zombie aspect, which meant little to the children, but about the topic of war and the focus on a violent military.

Yet not interfering with the children's representation of violence allowed their drawing to act as a documentation of their thinking, and through this activity, to make explicit in the external world something that was living in the children's consciousness. When violent play emerges from consciousness it can at least be studied, investigated; if it remains internal, no one knows the effects it produces on the psyche. To tell the child to stop shuts down communication between adult and child and all the possibilities that open out from sharing a part of ourselves with others. This is Carol Anne's interpretation; but, of course, there are many other viewpoints on this issue (e.g., Bergen 1994; Levin & Carlsson Paige 2005). In addition, because the imagined is not real, children maintain control and feel safe to play (Hall 2010; Paley 2005).

But more was going on in global events than our discussion so far acknowledges. The Zombie World project occurred between January and June of 2011, at the same time as the uprising and consequent war in Libya. Some 11 families in the building of 112 apartments above the child care center were affected directly by this war. Barbara Bigelow, the center director, says the tension and worry in the building was palpable. We do not know the extent to which the children—sensitive to images on television, YouTube, and other social media, and the worries and tension of the adults around them—were acting out those tensions in their invented world. But the violence was a fact of the real, external world they were indirectly experiencing. We also recognize that both fantasy play and drawing can be safe contexts for exploring power, control, and aggression (Dyson 1997; Hall 2010; Paley 1986).

Taking Zombie World Outside the Center

Three months of drawing, inventing, cutting, and taping had not slowed the boys' passion for their project. As Matthew shared the project with other staff members, Justin, a part-time student at the Nova Scotia College of Art and Design (NSCAD) and someone intrigued by visual art, was drawn into observing and participating in it. As mentioned above, Matthew and Justin had decided they wanted to cultivate stronger relations between the children and the local community. Justin suggested field trips to NSCAD for an exchange with students at the college. The children could share their creation of Zombie World, and the adult students could share their paintings and sculpture.

Justin gained permission from both institutions and from the children's parents to invite the group of six children most involved with Zombie World to visit NSCAD weekly to exchange in dialogue with the students in one of his courses. Between May and July the children visited the NSCAD painting studio, brought parts of Zombie World to share, and listened to the art students describe their own work. The visiting children began to grasp the notion of a *critique*—the sharing of impressions, interpretations, thoughts, and techniques in response to a created work. These exchanges were authentic and respectful on both sides, with the adult students sometimes astonished at the children's perceptions. One instance, for example, concerned a young woman who had painted a figure that her classmates did not understand. However, one of the children from Libya understood immediately: "It's about war, isn't it." The exchange with adult students also resulted in a change in how one child viewed himself: "Teachers always said my art was good, but I never believed it. I thought it was just stuff they said. But now I believe it."

Note: Before settling in Canada and cofounding the Nova Scotia College of Art and Design, Anna Leonowens (1831–1915) was more famously known as having been governess to the wives and children of the king of Siam (now called Thailand). Her story, first told in a best-selling 1944 book by Margaret Landon titled *Anna and the King of Siam*, was later adapted as the stage musical *The King and I* and for several movies.

Justin decided to share his gallery space for his final show with the children, making his own paintings an aesthetic reflection on the children's work and inviting the children into discussions with a curator to consider how the Zombie World material should be shown to others for best effect.

The Anna Leonowens Gallery (see Note) is a storefront art space belonging to NSCAD, open to the public, that offers shows of student work. In July the children's creation of Zombie World was installed for a week alongside Justin's paintings. Justin sent an invitation to the center community to visit the exhibit, and families attended the opening event and visited during the week of the installation. Unquestionably, seeing their creation displayed in a location outside the child care center in the larger community had a noticeable effect on the boys, and their pride in their activity was affirmed.

The children, accustomed to fundraising for things they want to do, have developed a sort of entrepreneurial spirit, and spontaneously shifted their assembly line process to make clay zombie figures—50 of them—that they thought they could sell at the art gallery. This unprompted shift to a different medium of representation was comfortable, we think, because the children were accustomed to using many different materials and believed in their freedom to try out the idea. (However, when they saw the little clay pieces arranged in the gallery, they decided they liked them too much to put them on sale.)

Zombie Contagion

Use of the zombie schema was spreading among the boys in the center. Without invitation from the adults, children in the senior classroom (for 3- to 5-year-olds) began drawing it. Even the 3-year-olds showed an interest: Repeatedly, children in the senior classroom adopted the older boys' schema for "zombie"—the X in a rectangle—in many forms, as if the children's desire was to participate in this shared creation belonging to older children. In September, when Zombie World was returned from the gallery to hang on the wall of the studio at the center, the younger children wanted to add to it, and showed absolute confidence in making drawings and taping them to the larger construction, as they had learned the after-school children did. The older boys did not seem to mind, tolerating these approximations, in colored paper and loose lines, added to the bottom of their highly detailed work.

Reflections

What Did the Term "Zombie" Mean to the Children?

For many educators, the topic of zombies is worrisome: Why would we support children in spending so much time on such a topic? When the teachers first showed Carol Anne the children's work in April 2011, she asked Matthew

and Justin, "What's the children's notion of a zombie? What does it mean to them?" In fact, Pete and Todd's idea for "a post-apocalyptic zombie newscast in comic book form" only lasted one day. That was the sole reference to an "apocalypse" and to our adult concept of zombies as "the walking dead." Instead, the children took up this new word in a playful way, naming characters using it (Zomboy, Zombaby, Zomcook, Zomqueen, and so forth) and otherwise associating *zombie* with aliens, spaceships, submarines, and eventually, the military. With the invention of their representative schema for "zombie," the term came to mean, for the children, any figure drawn using it. The schema itself became a vehicle for two things: for projecting whatever the child who was drawing wished to project (from zombie pets to zombie money cannons, from Zomgirl, Queen of Zombies, to zombie turtles), and at the same time, a way to identify with the collective activity, making that child part of the group. Children joined the collective activity by imagining their little zombie character in some location and activity, creating additions and alterations to the basic schema that reflected their intentions.

For the children, use of the schema was identity enough to join the group, for it was sufficiently open and undefined to carry their invention. Encapsulated in their large drawing, the boys had created their own subculture within the center, a subculture that spread to groups of younger children. The little zombie figure was both an invitation to belong to the culture and permission to invent and create for that culture. The term *zombie* seemed to name their invented world, so we were less inclined to be concerned, for they had no sense, that we could find, of adult meanings of the term *zombie*. We were more concerned about the militarism.

The Windhorse Effect

The children created in their drawing a landscape in which their imaginations were free to roam, to invent, and to communicate with one another. They invented ways of interconnecting ideas and inventions—both physically, through the device of taping together, and imaginatively, through tunnels and tubes, doorways and portals. Thus were they creating an imagined community, reflecting both what was on their minds (war) and what was imagined as fun for their invention—parachuting turtles, an anti gravity room, monsters, money. The freedom to play at the imagined and to share it joyfully with each other created a shared community of activity among the after-school boys that carried them for six months, then leapt to another classroom, where its influence was felt the entire following year.

This firestorm of positive energy for creating, something that Carol Anne calls the "windhorse effect," is a major consequence, in her view, of emergent curriculum. This effect occurs whenever children understand in their bones that their own good ideas will be accepted and supported by their teachers. In contexts where children have had multiple experiences of this support since they were very young, and understand that their families will also be interested in their efforts alongside their teachers, and where links with the community beyond the center are such that the children have confidence in their ideas, then their creativity explodes. When the children's positive energy is activated, they are flooded with ideas for invention. Love of the work, positive affect arising from their own creating, drives their activity.

Adults are invariably astonished at what young children so energized can design and produce, a fact witnessed by the international response to the Reggio Emilia experience (Edwards, Gandini, & Forman 2012). As Loris Malaguzzi, the Reggio leader from the 1960s into the 1990s, said:

> Once children are helped to perceive themselves as authors or inventors, once they are helped to discover the pleasure of inquiry, their motivation and interest explode. (Gandini 2012, 44)

We might note that this explosion of self-organized activity is what complexity theory predicts in living ecologies. Essential qualities of complex systems are unpredictability, the self-organization of elements within the system, and the emergence of something new—something greater than the sum of the parts (Capra 2002; Davis & Sumara 1997; Gleick 1987). Whether it be physics, biology, neuroscience, or mathematics, these features of complex systems have been confirmed repeatedly in multiple disciplines (Khattar 2009). The presence of *emergence* in a child care center, for Carol Anne, is an indication that the environment is a complex ecology—rich enough, responsive enough, to allow space for the creative energy of living creatures to make their own responses. These responses, of course, can be positive or negative, and occur irrespective of ethical concerns. But the fact of emergence, if the environment allows authentic responses, is undeniable.

Handling Representations of Violence

Carol Anne interprets Matthew's change in practice—from shutting down communication with children about drawings of violence to supporting its representation—as a development in his own aesthetic responsiveness. In her view, *aesthetic responsiveness* is the foundational disposition in the adult that allows emergent curriculum to expand. Aesthetic responsiveness means showing attitudes toward children of

- Authenticity—owning one's own reactions, such as worry about a topic
- Attentiveness—listening carefully, creating a suspension in time
- Appreciation—a capacity to embrace what happens, not to withdraw or block a relationship
- Empathy—a capacity to feel with others

Matthew was able to extend his appreciation for the children's chosen topic, acknowledging the terrific tension for himself in doing so, and suspended his response long enough to observe what was happening for the children. This suspension of response allows a breathing space in which teachers may investigate and study events, and share interpretations with others. We find that documentation (placeholding events in image and text so they may be studied)—helps teachers create this space of suspension. When dialogue is broadened in this way, out toward others, toward parents and community also, both the tension and the responsibility for responding become shared, and exchange may continue. Suspending judgment sustains relationships. Out of this suspension a stronger quality of responsiveness becomes possible.

But this change in Matthew's responsiveness is not to be confused with a permissiveness that allows children to engage in nasty behavior toward others. There were occasions that did require his intervention. During lunch, for example, he might hear a child try to coerce another, saying, "If you don't give me your chair [place for lunch], you're off the cutting team this afternoon." Matthew intervened with words such as, "I suggest you not use Zombie World to try to manipulate other children: I won't let that happen." Such intensity in the children shows the emotional power the project sustained for them, their intense desire to be part of it, and contexts in which the adults did contain that power.

Expanding Relations Through Community Connections

Matthew and Justin both hold a value that aims to make children and their voices more visible and accepted in public areas of our city. On their visit to Reggio Emilia, they were struck by the contrast between that Italian city and the expectations of our city of Halifax. The act of taking a small group of children to join a university painting class was, as Matthew put it at the time, "a small step in the right direction." And interestingly, Justin found the adult students more hesitant to share their point of view than were the children. Because of the work the boys had done with Justin at the center, they were able to talk about elements such as line and texture, surprising the adult students. One interesting result of this interchange was that a faculty member at NSCAD wrote a proposal for a grant to bring adult art students and children into a context where they might work together, and she proposes inviting children from our center as the first group of participants. We are heartened to learn that other institutions also show interest in communication between children and adults in contexts outside school and home.

Justin says a program goal is to see children's design work as part of the public sphere:

> "We want a public space—in the Public Gardens or Point Pleasant Park, for instance—so children's work can be seen, so there is respect for children. We want to bring the community together to see that children are citizens of this place."

Matthew and Justin see the interest of a member of the provincial legislature as a step in the direction of that goal. After attending Peter Green Hall Children's Centre's 45th Anniversary fundraising gala, where documentation of children's activity past and present was exhibited, including Zombie World, the legislator asked to have it displayed in her constituency office for several months later in the year.

In contrast, a less successful occasion was when the children drew maps with chalk on sidewalks in the neighborhood. This instance of children's participation in life outside the center was not well accepted by the neighbors, who saw it as graffiti and demanded that the children clean it up. The children scrubbed down the sidewalks, and the teachers documented the incident, including a narrative with photos and text in the exhibit at the gala. We see ourselves at the beginning of a long process attempting to build stronger roles and visibility for children in our city.

Differences Between Male and Female Teachers?

Do male teachers respond differently than female teachers to the interests and activities of children in child care? And in particular, to boys? The possibility arose when the Zombie World project was first shown to female staff. They didn't like it. They didn't like it especially for its depiction of war and violence. Several told Carol Anne that when they were first introduced to the wall of interconnected drawings they "just didn't get it." What didn't they get? They said they did not see "the depth in it." In Carol Anne's view, what the female teachers did not see was the

- Depth of the children's thinking
- Highly elaborate detail in their drawings
- Boys' intense stimulation to keep on inventing
- Cleverness of the taping together of individual pieces as a strategy for holding together a community of thought and feeling in a landscape
- Way the landscape—a map to a world—contained the thoughts and inventions of many children simultaneously
- Ease with which the children accepted ideas from the group of participants
- Self-organization the children voluntarily imposed on themselves to mass-produce figures that could be moved about from one part of the landscape to another
- Positive energy communally shared and directed toward designing and making
- Sheer love of the activity

All this complexity was invisible to the female teachers because of their feelings about the theme of violent war.

Was Zombie World a context showing differences in male and female teachers in child care? Or was Matthew and Justin's tolerance for war fantasy in the boys' invented world a genderless responsiveness to children's interests? The early childhood literature demonstrates little difference between male and female teachers in their effects upon children: For example, Carrington and colleagues (2007) note that the gender of teachers had little effect on "children's level of academic engagement or the perceived quality of their classroom experiences" (p. 411) for 7- and 8-year-olds, as did Sokal and colleagues (2005). Shears (2010) points out that "much of the literature does not support education gains where there is a male teacher" (p. 68). The classic study by Gold and Reiss (1982) found "the hypothesis that male teachers reduce boys' problems in school does not receive much support empirically or theoretically" (p. 493). Sumsion's (2005) more recent review and research also finds no difference. A contrasting view comes from Dee (2006), who did find a difference, but in research with much older, grade 8 students. Of course, that the literature finds no educative difference based on gender does not deny the fact that there may be differences between the views of males and females.

What We Learned

A controversial activity for us, Zombie World was a child-initiated project that emerged in the after-school classroom but came to permeate the entire center. This work continued in the senior classroom, among the 3- to 5-year-olds, the following year—the zombie schema became a seemingly permanent aspect of the children's local culture.

We learned much from the event. We learned from the literature that the initial difference between male and female teachers' appreciation of the project likely did not make a difference in effects on children. We learned that violence in children's fantasy play, as captured in drawing, reveals children's thinking about aspects of the real world. We saw in that play children's belief in the power of the military to act and the power of groups to generate money and wealth. In retrospect, we can see this project as one in which the children were showing us the importance of being strong, in control, and powerful. A year later, while discussing the project, we realized the children had not drawn anyone being hurt, though someone did draw an infirmary with nurses and stretchers.

We learned that parts of the community will appreciate children's work and presence in more public forums, even while other parts resist such presence.

And finally, we learned to continue to trust the remarkable energy of the children to create out of their group intentions, to design a culture that was both invention and reflection of the global world. The windhorse of energy beneath their creative production once again illustrates the extraordinary capacities of children, if adults will but listen.

Travis Wright

Zombie World—
Not Just for Children

Z ombie World is a powerful testament to children's ability to create, convene, and challenge adults and their community. Such is the magic of an emergent approach and bearing witness to children's journeys. Carol Anne Wien, Matthew Sampson, Justin West, and Barbara Bigelow do an excellent job of capturing the multiple layers of meaning that are at play in any one moment in early childhood settings. They highlight the potential for both understanding and misunderstanding as we seek to interpret the languages of childhood. They point out for readers the fragile balance between teaching from hope and teaching from fear, acknowledging risk while recognizing children's resistance and resilience. Following I will discuss the importance and promise of honoring the children's lives and navigating this complexity in our classrooms and relationships with them.

In Zombie World, we see the tension between what the children were doing and what adults feared their actions meant. What children seem to be talking about at times challenges their teachers to see how the children are talking about it. Although the story lines in Zombie World frequently involve soldiers, guns, and warmongering turtles, the children work collaboratively and nonviolently to weave their tales. The experience of creating something together, sitting alongside each other every afternoon for months, and having the teachers celebrate their creations will have far a greater impact on who the children become than will the "apocalyptic" content of their work. Had the teachers decided to censor the children's emergent conversation, the children would likely have felt frustrated, dismissed, and silenced. As we have become all too painfully aware, those are the emotions that lead to violence. Perhaps ironically, not allowing children to talk about their darker emotions is the very way to feed them.

As educators, we spend a lot of our energy considering how we might improve what we do for and with children. However, sometimes we miss the "bigness" of childhood if we do not also allow children to call forth things in us, helping us to identify ways in which we might grow and to imagine different possibilities for ourselves and the world. In our efforts to protect children from the world that we fear for them or the world that we are afraid they might create, we sometimes fail to recognize their resilience and resistance. These very same fears, of losing control or of changing our minds, may also get in the way of our relating to children, our ability to see the world through their eyes. We might miss opportunities to pick up on their commentary about the world in which they live.

Interestingly, in this chapter, though we hear from adults what they learned from Zombie World and what they think Zombie World meant to children, we do not hear from the children themselves. As is frequently the case, the adults in the community seemed to clash with each other about the children's work. Yet, as evidenced by children's comfort in discussing their work with art students and community members, the children were more than capable of sharing their process and intentions. I wonder how Zombie World might have transpired differently if teachers had shared their questions and fears about the work with the children? Opening such a dialogue might have allowed both the children and the adults to broaden their perspectives on each other and themselves. Such open, honest conversations with children have provided me with some of the most powerful growing experiences of my life. Indeed, children may carry more than themselves on their "wind-horses" (Wien 2008).

Children frequently create and inhabit worlds with far more wisdom and insight than we allow them. These special places frequently mirror the way they see us, but also the possibilities they imagine for us. In a world where the most visible examples of collective action are rooted in violence—war, sports, and divisive politics, for example—how can children represent coming together without the pretense and props of war? At a time when children are far too frequently assessed, measured, and compared, how else can they create their imagined world but with assembly lines?

Nevertheless, the children's motivation for their work is collaborative, inviting, and generous. The children accepted the imprecise contributions of the "little kids," made space for the Zombie Queen's hearts, and were willing to discuss with strangers their intent. While the adults spent much time voicing their concern about the "eruption of violence in the midst of the project," it took them more than a year to notice that in Zombie World there was actually no fighting, only nursing wards for those who had been wounded. And the children are boys. Though dominant stereotypes and society's expectations frequently cast young boys as aggressive and self-focused, establishing dominance through bullying and threats, these boys provide a different image of masculinity. Instead of perpetuating violence, perhaps the children resist it, expanding their and our notions of how they might relate beyond or in spite of the weapons and postures adults expect them to hold.

Indeed, Zombie World is not just for children, and is perhaps their powerful critique of the world that we inhabit, that we are creating for them. As evidenced by the energy generated among the children, their teachers, and the broader community, this consuming effort meant something. This something grabbed hold and did not let go. When and how do we blindly perpetuate stereotypes and wounds from our pasts? How might we begin to sit together, imagine new possibilities for ourselves, and tape together a shared vision for the future that allows enough room for everyone to draw her or his own type of picture? And, as the children taught us in Zombie World, if we join with them in creating this space, there will much additional magic to discover.

....

Travis Wright, EdD, is an assistant professor of early childhood education at the University of Wisconsin–Madison. His research focuses on teaching young children growing up in challenging circumstances.

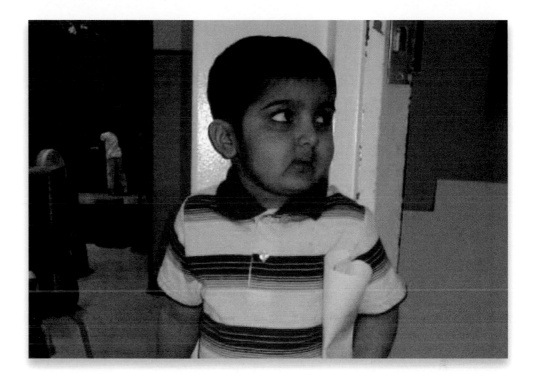

Chapter 10

**Carol Anne Wien,
Bobbi-Lynn Keating,
Justin West, and
Barbara Bigelow**

Aaqib at the Center

This is the story of a 4-year-old boy named Aaqib (pronounced *Akeeb*) who came to Peter Green Hall Children's Centre in remission from a rare form of brain cancer that had been diagnosed when he was 18 months old. The story does not have a happy ending in which he is miraculously cured. You may wonder why we would include the topic of a seriously ill child in a book on emergent curriculum. It was Elizabeth Jones who pointed out that "emergent curriculum is what happens" . . . that life experience should be part of a program (Jones 2012; Jones & Nimmo 1994).

Following six major surgeries and countless chemotherapy and radiation treatments, Aaqib's right side and his legs were weak, so while he could walk—crossing a room with surprising speed—he tired easily. His lungs were damaged by radiation treatments. He spoke in two- and three-word utterances in English in a family where two languages were spoken at home. But he was recovering.

Aaqib's father, Zahoor Khan, had taught at a medical college in Saudi Arabia and immigrated to Canada with his family to undertake a doctorate in engineering at Dalhousie University, in Halifax, Nova Scotia. Halifax was also desirable because of the advanced cancer care available at its IWK Children's Hospital. During the family's first two years living in Peter Green Hall, Aaqib was too ill to be in child care, but the staff and children at the center all knew him, as he accompanied his family to drop off his younger brother. A charismatic presence, Aaqib wore sunglasses and rode his tricycle through the hallways, greeting everyone with pleasure. Now, after 2½ years of illness, his parents wanted him to have a chance to play with other children. His teachers, thinking ahead to school, wanted to help him develop a social life outside hospitals, a life that included friendship with peers.

In September 2010, when Aaqib was 4, he was welcomed into the center's senior classroom with 20 other children (ages 3½ to 5) and three teachers. What happens for the other children, families, and teachers when such a child and his family become an integral part of daily life in their center? Would he play with the other children? Would the children accept him? How would he do without his mother, who had been with him constantly at home and in the hospital, especially given that she gave birth to a third son on the day Aaqib began the program?

Looking back on their time with Aaqib, assistant director and teacher Bobbi-Lynn Keating says, "It seemed routine in the beginning but would turn out to be life-changing for all of us."

Aaqib Enters the Classroom

From the moment Aaqib entered the classroom, the children both engaged with him as a peer and made their own observations:

"Why does Aaqib have lines [scars] on his head?"

"Why does Aaqib take medicine every day?"

"Why does Aaqib cough so much?"

This center's approach is to be both open and honest with children, and the teachers offered accurate information or asked the children what they themselves thought.

"He has lines on his head because he had a lump inside that the doctors had to remove."

"He takes medicine every day to make him stronger."

"He coughs because his lungs are damaged."

Aaqib was a fast learner, settling in to enjoy, as staff observation notes say, some "excellent work times" during which he was very engaged, cutting with scissors for 20 minutes, engaging with peers rather than teachers, making friends with classmates Jake and Tony. He spontaneously helped other children, opening the laundry bin for one child and climbing on the table at lunch to pour milk for another. He completed an obstacle course one day, crawling through the tunnel with ease, then said, "All done. Sleep," and his teacher, Bobbi, introduced a quiet area where he could rest.

But this gives an incomplete image, for Aaqib's entry in September was dramatic: He did not want to stay or have Sumera, his mother, leave him, and showed tremendous strength in resisting being in the program. He constantly wanted to leave the room, for example, and would simply walk out the door. Bobbi and teacher Justin West had to use every strategy in their repertoire to keep him in the room. Worse, when unable to leave as he wished, he had outbursts of kicking, scratching, hitting, and pulling the hair of the adults that astonished everyone.

Although the teachers offered constant reassurance to Sumera that their separation would become easier, they were themselves struggling. Aaqib constantly wanted little things contrary to what they were, and engaged the staff in power struggles over them. Bobbi describes what it was like:

"If the door was open, he wanted it closed. If the window was closed, he wanted it open. If the children were sitting for circle, he wanted to stand. I never thought of him as sick [during this time], he was so stubborn."

In contrast, he was kind toward other children; he enjoyed them, never took things from them or had any outbursts in his interactions with the children. Because of the tremendous difficulty of his entry, Carol Anne Wien asked Bobbi and Justin whether they liked Aaqib. Bobbi says,

"Oh, yes. We loved him. We bonded right away. He had this quiet humor beyond what you would expect in a child. He loved the songs, he loved books, he loved Jake, he loved Tony, and the other kids loved him. They did everything to make him happy."

Jake sat and played with him. Tony would find materials for him. Bobbi continues,

"Even if Jake was doing something else, if Aaqib coughed, Jake would go get his water bottle from Aaqib's locker—he knew he needed a drink—then return to what he was doing [across the room]."

Once Tony saw Aaqib hitting Bobbi and intervened, offered him toys, saying, "No hitting, you can't hit a teacher."

Hopkins (2002) notes that, "Aggressive behaviors and temper tantrums are common in children who feel out of control" (p. 42). And Aaqib was a child who had endured the suffering and fear of extreme intrusion in his body. During his many

hospitalizations, he had nonetheless learned ways to sustain a sort of agency in the face of his suffering. As Bobbi and the other teachers learned later,

"When a nurse came to one side of the hospital bed to give him a needle, Aaqib might say to his mother, 'No.' And his mother would tell the nurse that Aaqib wanted her to come to the other side of the bed, use the other arm. . . . He ran that room."

Anthropologist Bluebond-Langner (1978) writes that children as young as 3 years of age know when they are seriously ill: "Children possess a self, and are, therefore, purposeful, willful individuals capable of organizing their own behavior toward others" (p. 7). Aaqib's mother interpreted and carried out his intentions, giving her son small moments of control in the face of what he had to endure.

Although it was not apparent, because we did not yet know his relationships in the hospital, in retrospect we think that Aaqib was using the same strategy when he came to the center that had worked for him in the hospital, and was surprised and frustrated when it did not work in the child care setting. There are many possible additional hypotheses for his classroom outbursts—the rupture in his bond with his mother, who so supported him in making his world work; the expectation that he act independently, when he had had no previous independent life; the sudden appearance of a new baby in his family—these are but a few. Another might be displaced rage at his illness, acted out in a place that was not life-threatening. According to Waechter (1984), seriously ill children may feel anger and, "because it is frightening to be angry at people on whom they depend," may direct that anger elsewhere (p. 57).

By the end of September, Aaqib was in all-out rebellion, with tremendous resistance to routines and enormous power struggles over tiny things such as keeping his shoes on, a center safety policy. Yet arrival and nap times had become easier. Four teachers worked with him in 15-minute shifts to prevent their own exhaustion. Justin says, "He put us to an extreme test." The struggle was devastating for Bobbi and Justin, normally highly successful teachers; but Carol Anne thinks it was also a marvelous show of Aaqib's strength, a kind of rage for some control over his life, an insistence that he had the power to have an impact on his environment.

He also had some excellent days, dressing the baby dolls with great gentleness and enjoying the challenge of buttons and snaps. He was engaged at circle time, laughing uproariously at the song "Sticky, Sticky Bubble Gum" and the book *Good Night, Gorilla* (by Peggy Rathmann). He loved painting, Thomas the Train, playing with teddy bear counters, throwing and dropping objects from the edge of a table and watching them fall.

Thus his and the teachers' adjustment was progressing, but in late October Aaqib was again hospitalized with lung problems. When he returned home, doctors told his parents he was too ill to be around children all day. In November and December the children saw him in the hallways, and chatted with him and his family when they came to pick up his brother. Aaqib was on oxygen.

Extending the Caring Community

In January Aaqib had a severe crisis with his lungs and was put in a coma and on a ventilator. Center staff visited from time to time to support his family. Bobbi said, "We did not know if he would wake up; but Aaqib is a fighter, and he did."

At this point Bobbi asked center director Barbara Bigelow if she would approach his mother to ask whether the children might also visit Aaqib in the hospital. Sumera, who was essentially living there now with her infant son, extended an open invitation. Bobbi began taking small groups of four to six children for visits to the hospital, which is within walking distance of the center.

What did the hospital doctors and nurses think about the visits, given that Aaqib was too ill to be around children all day? In fact, they were welcoming, answering the children's questions about machines and inviting them to listen through the stethoscopes. Dr. Gerri Frager, head of Pediatric Palliative Care at the hospital, told us medical staff typically are happy to have children visit, provided they have support, someone they can talk to about any concerns.

Aaqib would see the children's faces in the observation window of his room as they arrived and call out, "Friends!" When they entered, he insisted his mother serve them juice. When she poured apple juice, he said, "No, red juice," his favorite. During the visits Sumera would sometimes slip away for a few moments of respite.

Bobbi says of the decision to take children to visit, "We felt that Aaqib might not be with us but he's part of our classroom. How can we still hold him as a member of our community?" One way they found was to videotape circle time, with the children singing his favorite songs such as "Ten in the Bed" and "Sticky, Sticky Bubble Gum" and reading *Good Night, Gorilla*. Five children brought the videotape on one of their visits and watched it with Aaqib. He laughed and performed the actions to the songs, and that made everyone laugh. His mother later said he watched the video every day, and wanted his doctors and nurses to see it.

Another way they could hold him in the center's community was to give friends access to each other. Bobbi says, "The children who were his friends had a right to see him, and Aaqib to see them, to be with each other. If he were 40, you wouldn't deny friends access, and we thought it would be healing for him and for those he would leave." Once when they arrived to find a team of doctors and nurses in Aaqib's room, Bobbi offered to come back later, but the doctors said, "No, your being here is important."

For Aaqib's family—alone in a country far from home—the center offered an acceptance of their situation and a friendship that brought them into the midst of the local community of parents. Barb says,

> "We have a strong interconnection between the families and the center. Perhaps this is because many of our families are away from their homes and sometimes we become their 'extended family.' Perhaps it is because we are all in the same building together. The bond that develops feels like a natural support system that is reciprocal. For example, the center supports families in many ways. Some of the staff provide child care after hours, we provide space for families for celebrations, parents may seek advice with parenting questions.

> "At the same time, parents offer us their trust in our abilities to make good decisions about the education of their children and they support us through fundraising, volunteering, donating, computer assistance, and so on. As a result of these kinds of interactions, respect develops between the families and the center in much the same way as we respect children in our care."

His dad, Zahoor, would often stop in the center's office with updates on Aaqib's health and show Barb photos on his cell phone of Aaqib in the hospital. Barb also phoned Sumera for updates. His younger brother's teacher, Elizabeth, and Barb visited the hospital regularly, and Elizabeth would look after Sumera's baby so Sumera could have a break. Some parents cooked food that staff took with them when visiting the hospital. Barb says, "We offered ourselves to the family, but I think what they appreciated most was the visits from the children. Aaqib loved Bobbi and waited for their visits."

Will Aaqib Survive?

In late winter it was clear that Aaqib was not a candidate for a lung transplant. It was also clear he would not be returning to the classroom, and the children were disturbed when his teachers removed Aaqib's name from his locker. By early April, Aaqib's condition was grave. He was not going to be able to fight illness much longer. Bobbi recalls,

"The children noticed on their visits that the tubes and machines were bigger. His mother would call Barb to say whether it was a good day for the children to visit: Some days we couldn't visit because he was too sick. One day I overheard children discussing Aaqib as they read books in the library. I sat down with them to listen to what they had to say."

Jake: "I think he's going to die, but he should stay with doctors and have ice cream."

Tony: "He won't die. I know! After he gets all better . . . he will never get better . . . and he has to get better."

Malik: "I don't think Aaqib's going to die; he's going to get better next week."

Jake: "I don't think he will. They have to put his pieces back fast. They have to sew it with thread. He will still get a line [scar] when they do it fast."

Bobbi: "How would you feel if Aaqib died?"

Children: "We'd be angry." (Nadine begins to cry.)

Jake: "I think she is crying because she is thinking if Aaqib dies she will never see him again and she would be sad."

Lily: "If he died, he will never play or make playdough with us."

We see in the children's mixed reactions—of thinking he might die and that "he has to get better"—the same anxiety and disbelief that adults feel in such a situation. How can dying really happen to someone we love who belongs to us? We see in Jake's theory that both doctors and ice cream have a beneficial effect an implied hope that they might continue to do so. Tony succinctly phrases everyone's feeling, both that Aaqib cannot get better and that he must.

Bobbi's question, direct and simple, turns the children to consider their own feelings. Jake was Aaqib's closest friend. When Bobbi heard Jake imply that the doctors would have to work very quickly, she knew he understood that Aaqib's situation was very serious. His understanding made her very emotional, and she suddenly understood her own and the rest of the staff's responsibility to share whatever happened with other center families, to lead in the response, if Aaqib should die. But how far should they go, how far should they take their involvement?

In late April Bobbi and children were visiting each day. Children chose to go, including new members of the senior classroom who had just moved up from the junior class: They knew Aaqib's situation was the most important aspect of their community at this time.

On Friday, April 29, Aaqib had a very hard night, experiencing a cardiac episode. Bobbi recalls,

"His mom called and said that we probably shouldn't go visit. Aaqib was tired, and they had a friend coming to take some family pictures. Maybe the children should come after the weekend.

"On Monday, May 2nd, we got children ready after lunch to go to the hospital. On our way out, Barb stopped us and motioned us to come back. I knew then, Aaqib had died. The hospital had called. We returned to the classroom to tell the children, but they could already sense it. The children had a lot of questions, so as a 'family' we discussed it all and shared our emotions and our feelings."

When Bobbi told the children Aaqib had died, Jake said,

"I knewed [sic] you were going to say that."

Other children had different responses:

"How do you know that?"

Bobbi: "Do you remember all the doctors and nurses in his room? They couldn't fix what was wrong with Aaqib."

"I can't believe that."

"I will think about it but won't be sad. Lots of people are still alive, it's only one person that is dead."

"His mom will cry because she really loves him. That is why she will cry."

"When you're dead, you can't come back."

"You put all the things you loved about him, you hold them in the palm of your hand, and put them in your heart."

Even when death is expected, its sudden presence as fact is a shock, and we see the children's disbelief, just as we recognize our own. We also see an attempt at a sort of rational perspective in the view that "lots of other people are still alive." Perhaps most remarkable is a child's empathy for Aaqib's mother.

The literature on the development of children's understanding of death says that many children grasp the three most basic aspects of death—*irreversibility* (death cannot be undone), *inevitability* (everyone will someday die), and *cessation* (stop in life-defining characteristics)—between ages 5 and 7 (Slaughter 2005; Sood et al. 2006; Speece & Brent 1984; Vianello & Marin 1989; Willis 2002). Bobbi remains firm in her belief that in spite of their young age (3½–5) many of the children in the senior classroom *did* understand that death is irreversible, that Aaqib could not come back. This literature also recognizes that young children may develop a precocious understanding of death when they experience it close at hand. When we talked with his parents, Sumera said,

"I learned from him—it was inspiring: He was happy with whatever he could do within the circle of his limits."

His father said,

"We spent three years in hospital with him but he never seemed like a patient. Even his last morning, he was still himself. I asked him, 'Do you need anything?' . . . 'Watermelon.' . . . So I got a sliver from the fridge. Then he asked for his grandmothers and we phoned. He asked to see several nurses, and he asked for Bobbi, to read him *Good Night, Gorilla*."

In fact, Bobbi later went to see Aaqib, his body washed and dressed in the hospital, and found herself reading *Good Night, Gorilla* to him one last time.

Grieving for Aaqib and Celebrating His Life

This chaotic day required that the teachers also support the other families. Parents arrived to pick up their children, who would run across the room, jump in their laps, and say, "Guess what, Mommy: Aaqib died today." For the other parents the news was harrowing, evoking their own immediate empathy for a parent losing a child. One child said to her mother, "It's okay, you can cry. Bobbi cried today, too," and went and got her mother a tissue. Another mother reported that her daughter asked her several times over the next week whether she was sad and wanted to cry.

Dr. Frager met with staff and parents that evening at the center. (Some staff found it too difficult to participate in this meeting, fearing their own loss of self-control.) The parents wanted to be supportive of Aaqib's family, but were unsure what to do. Many thanked the teachers for allowing their children to participate in such an experience. And while the parents felt helpless, they trusted the teachers would know what to do for their children. Because Aaqib's family required separate spaces for men and women to grieve, the center offered his classroom to the family.

In the days that followed, the children in the center repeatedly wanted to sing Aaqib's favorite songs and read *Good Night, Gorilla*. His younger brother moved from the juniors room (for children 2½ to 3½ years old) to the senior classroom, and his family was happy he was there with the children who knew his big brother and could grieve with him. They said Aaqib would have been proud of his little brother moving up.

Bobbi and Barb watched parents not knowing what to do when they encountered Sumera bringing Aaqib's younger brother into the senior classroom. There were photographs of Aaqib all around, and Barb and Bobbi found themselves working hard to create interactions in a situation other parents found difficult. We see the necessity of creating a classroom supportive of the emotions caused by death (Hopkins 2002) and the positive ways Aaqib and his family were acknowledged.

Aaqib's fifth birthday would have been July 14. Barb says she found it very difficult to consider celebrating his birthday, but thought it might be a way to bring the community of families together, and give the other families a way to acknowledge Aaqib's family and share in something about him with them.

Bobbi talked about it with the children:

"The children made several suggestions . . . that Aaqib must be in the sky, and for his birthday we should send him balloons."

The center and Aaqib's family planned the celebration together. On his birthday, staff and parents arrived, some with a single balloon, some with clusters; and Aaqib's family arrived with his favorite red juice and cake for everyone. But our government regulations for child care dictate that no cake will be served in a licensed center. What to do? The cake cannot be served in the child care center; and the cake, a gesture of hospitality from the family, cannot be refused. The cake was set up in the center's studio, where the family could serve it themselves after the balloon release, and families could come in as they were leaving and share a few moments with Aaqib's family, taking cake with them. This celebration of Aaqib's life offered other families an opportunity to show their support to his family, to offer their condolences and recognition of his life within their family, and recognized the family's place in the community of the center.

Reflections

This was an experience that came to us, not one that any family or center would choose. To bear the death of a loved and dear child is beyond what anyone could describe as conventional practice in child care. To Carol Anne, the manner in which the center met the challenge signifies a further development in their practice that goes far beyond conventional notions of

emergent curriculum. It signifies what practice might become when the community of such a center is able to embrace difficult knowledge.

For Carol Anne, one of the astonishing aspects of the Reggio-inspired practice that Peter Green Hall has developed is that the teachers have taught themselves how to appreciate the unbearable. Aaqib was welcomed without question; and when his health worsened, the teachers did not withdraw from the situation, but faced the difficulty with courage. If taking children to visit Aaqib in hospital was unconventional, it was consistent with Bobbi's goal of keeping the children in communication, and with the center's goal of cultivating in authentic ways strong relations with parts of the community beyond the center. The context of serious difficulty was also, thus, an opportunity, a direction in their practice. I believe this appreciation for difficulty arises from the stance of *aesthetic responsiveness*— the listening, the empathy, the authenticity, and willingness to embrace life as it is—that the staff has learned over many years to show for others (Khattar & Wien 2012).

As a staff they have, over many years, learned that it is possible to undertake what seems impossible, or unbearably difficult, and to permit the center and each participant to be changed—both challenged and enriched—by the difficulty willingly invited into their programs. This stance is demonstrated by their leaders, Barb and Bobbi, and the staff rise to the occasion in a fierce commitment to their mission of offering respect and nurturance to all families. Barb says, "Families come to us and we develop strong relationships and so they trust us." I find that the center shows exceptional courage in facing the unknown realities of extreme difficulty, carrying a conscious commitment to honor their mission.

In Carol Anne's view, these teachers push the practice of child care and education beyond the boundaries of what we have known or thought possible, and this story exemplifies that aspect of their commitment. The emotional depth that is experienced among people who are coping with difficulty not only enriches relationships but also keeps experiences centered in what is deeply significant to being alive in the world. What is difficult can also generate much gratitude.

Carolyn Pope
Edwards and
Lella Gandini

A Welcoming Heart and Open Mind for All

"It seemed routine in the beginning, but would turn out to be life-changing for all of us."

"Aaqib at the Center" is the remarkable story of a child's fraught entry into a child care center, and then of his journey, alongside his own family, the center children and families, and caring medical personnel, as he eventually loses his battle with cancer and is remembered by those who have come to love him.

The chapter has many lessons for high-quality early childhood education and care and implications for the practice of teaching young children. From the opening sentences, the story demonstrates the way in which a preschool child can maintain force of personality and uniqueness even as his physical health deteriorates. In addition to Aaqib's courage and determination, the story reveals his eagerness to connect and make friends his own age. The account vividly confirms findings from the child development literature that from the beginning, children experience "peer hunger" and desire to belong to the life of a group. Aaqib's and his peers' capacities for friendship should give confidence to all of us in early education that the opportunities we provide are something that young children desire and appreciate.

One of the most striking aspects of the chapter is how the teachers created an effective emergent curriculum not only for Aaqib but also for all the other children and families in the program. The curriculum even extended to the adults encountered at the hospital, when the children and teachers visit Aaqib after he was too sick to attend preschool. The basis of their emergent planning is careful observation and listening: being attentive to the children's words, documenting them, and using empathy and knowledge to try to understand what they mean. This emotional attunement makes the children true participants in the complex drama of Aaqib's life and death. For example, when Aaqib's condition deteriorates to the point that the children become aware that he might die, the teachers listen and write down the words of the children. We see in the children's mixed reactions—thinking he might die but also that "he has to get better"—the same anxiety and disbelief that the adults feel. Yet, Aaqib unfortunately died, and here we should reflect on some of the children's words that teachers transcribed:

"I can't believe that."

"I will think about it but won't be sad. Lots of people are still alive, it's only one person that is dead."

"His mom will cry because she really loves him. That is why she will cry."

"When you're dead, you can't come back."

The authors ask, "How can dying really happen to someone we love who belongs to us?" How is it possible? The children try, in their different ways, to express their disbelief. We can note the depth of their responses as they try to cope with the loss. The children give the teachers and parents a hand in reaching out and being part of a community. Their symbolic communication—wanting to send balloons into the sky to touch Aaqib's spirit—suggests the significance of emotional language for human beings and the unexpectedly high intelligence and maturity that preschool children can reveal.

In multiple ways, the teachers do far more than manage a difficult situation; instead they reflect deeply together and create a series of growth and learning experiences for everyone. In response to an inviting attitude, as time passes and Aaqib's health declines, his mother generously allows the teachers to take small groups of children to visit him in the hospital. This is a reassuring learning experience for the children, who are welcomed with joy by their friend, his mother, and even by the extraordinarily wise doctors and nurses, who understand the value of having these young friends in their space at this point in Aaqib's life.

The chapter also reveals the importance of teachers being willing to take the risk of being honest with themselves and one another about their feelings. For example, the chapter describes frankly the lengthy struggle of Aaqib's transition into the center. Through observation and discussion, teachers came to understand that these difficulties are a power struggle on Aaqib's part, resulting from his need to have some control over his life. As a result, the teachers dig deeper, help one another, and invent creative strategies for supporting his transition.

This center is truly a welcoming place. The teachers respect the preferences of Aaqib's immigrant family without any overt resistance. For example, the center respects the family's cultural values about gender roles and their heartfelt wish to share a cake at the memorial ceremony held on the anniversary of Aaqib's birthday.

Loris Malaguzzi always asked us to start from the children to reformulate our roles as teachers. As he said, "We must give credit to the potential and the power that children possess. We must be convinced that children, like us, have stronger powers than those we have been told about, powers which we all possess, stronger potential than we give them credit for" (Rinaldi 1996). Problems in schools are less likely to arise when there is a high level of awareness and use of all the intelligences, abilities, and potentials that we possess.

....

Carolyn Pope Edwards, EdD, is a Willa Cather Professor at the University of Nebraska–Lincoln, where she teaches developmental psychology and early childhood education.

Lella Gandini, EdD, is Visiting Scholar 2007–2013 at Lesley University in Cambridge, Massachusetts, and Reggio Children U.S. Liaison for the Dissemination of the Reggio Emilia Approach.

References

Ambery, M.E. 1997. "Time for Franklin." *Young Children* 52 (4): 70–71.

Avery, J. 2013. "Artists at the Centre Project." Unpublished documentation. Hamilton, ON, Canada.

Batson, C.D., & L.L. Shaw. 1991. "Evidence for Altruism: Toward a Pluralism of Prosocial Motives." *Psychological Inquiry* 2 (2): 107–22.

Bergen, D. 1994. "Should Teachers Permit or Discourage Violent Play Themes?" *Childhood Education* 70 (5): 300–302.

Bluebond-Langner, M. 1978. *The Private Worlds of Dying Children.* Princeton, NJ: Princeton University Press.

Bredekamp, S., ed. 1987. *Developmentally Appropriate Practice in Early Childhood Programs Serving Children From Birth Through Age 8.* Expanded ed. Washington, DC: NAEYC.

Bredekamp, S., & C. Copple, eds. 1997. *Developmentally Appropriate Practice in Early Childhood Programs.* Rev. ed. Washington, DC: NAEYC.

Bresler, L. 2008. "The Music Lesson." Chap. 19 in *Handbook of the Arts in Qualitative Research: Perspectives, Methodologies, Examples and Issues,* eds. J.G. Knowles & A.L. Cole, 225–38. Thousand Oaks, CA: Sage.

Bruner, J. 1996. "A Little City Miracle." In *The Hundred Languages of Children: Narrative of the Possible,* ed. L. Malaguzzi. [catalogue to the exhibit]. Reggio Emilia, Italy: Municipality of Reggio Emilia.

Cadwell, L. 1997. *Bringing Reggio Emilia Home: An Innovative Approach to Early Childhood Education.* New York: Teachers College Press.

Cadwell, L.B. 2003. *Bringing Learning to Life: The Reggio Approach to Early Childhood.* New York: Teachers College Press.

Capra, F. 2002. *The Hidden Connection: Integrating the Biological, Cognitive, and Social Dimensions of Life into a Science of Sustainability.* New York: Doubleday.

Carrington, B., B. Francis, M. Hutchings, C. Skelton, B. Read, & I. Hall. 2007. "Does the Gender of the Teacher Really Matter? Seven-to-Eight-Year-Olds' Accounts of Their Interactions with Their Teachers." *Educational Studies* 33 (4): 397–413.

Churchill, W. 1947. Speech, House of Commons, November 11, 1947.

Connery, C., V. John-Steiner, & A. Marjanovic-Shane, eds. 2010. *Vygotsky and Creativity: A Cultural-Historical Approach to Play, Meaning Making and the Arts.* New York: Peter Lang.

Cooper, M. 2012. "Is Beauty a Way of Knowing?" In *The Hundred Languages of Children: The Reggio Emilia Experience in Transformation,* 3rd ed., eds. C. Edwards, L. Gandini, & G. Forman, 295–302. Santa Barbara, CA: Clio.

Copple, C., & S. Bredekamp, eds. 2009. *Developmentally Appropriate Practice in Early Childhood Programs Serving Children From Birth Through Age 8.* 3rd ed. Washington, DC: NAEYC.

Csikszentmihalyi, M. 1990. *Flow: The Psychology of Optimum Experience.* New York: Harper & Row.

Curtis, D., & M. Carter. 2003. *Designs for Living and Learning: Transforming Early Childhood Environments.* St. Paul, MN: Redleaf Press.

Curtis, D., & M. Carter. 2007. *Learning Together With Young Children: A Curriculum Framework for Reflective Teachers.* St. Paul, MN: Redleaf Press.

Dahlberg, G., P. Moss, & A. Pence. 2007. *Beyond Quality in Early Childhood Education and Care: Languages of Evaluation.* 2nd ed. New York: Routledge.

Damon, W. 1988. *The Moral Child: Nurturing Children's Natural Moral Growth.* New York: The Free Press.

Davis, B., & D. Sumara. 1997. "Cognition, Complexity, and Teacher Education." *Harvard Educational Review* 67 (1): 105–25.

Davoli, M., & G. Ferri. 2000. *Reggio Tutta: A Guide to the City by the Children.* Reggio Emilia, Italy: Reggio Children.

Dee, T.S. 2006. "The Why Chromosome: How a Teacher's Gender Affects Boys and Girls." *Education Next* 6 (4): 69–75. http://educationnext.org/files/ednext20064_68.pdf.

Delrio, G. 2012. "Our Responsibility Toward Young Children and Their Community." In *The Hundred Languages of Children: The Reggio Emilia Experience in Transformation,* 3rd ed., eds. C. Edwards, L. Gandini, & G. Forman, 81–88. Santa Barbara, CA: Praeger.

Detour, A., & M.E. Logue. 2011. "'You Be the Bad Guy': A New Role for Teachers in Supporting Children's Dramatic Play." *Early Childhood Research and Practice* 13 (1).

Dewey, J. 1934. *Art as Experience.* New York: Minton, Balch & Company.

Duckworth, E. 2006. *"The Having of Wonderful Ideas" and Other Essays on Teaching and Learning.* 3rd ed. New York: Teachers College Press.

Dyson, A. 1997. *Writing Superheroes: Contemporary Childhood, Popular Culture, and Classroom Literacy.* New York: Teachers College Press.

Edwards, C., L. Gandini, & G. Forman, eds. 1993. *The Hundred Languages of Children: The Reggio Emilia Approach to Early Childhood Education.* Norwood, NJ: Ablex.

Edwards, C., L. Gandini, & G. Forman, eds. 2012. *The Hundred Languages of Children: The Reggio Emilia Experience in Transformation.* 3rd ed. Santa Barbara, CA: Praeger.

Eisenberg, N. 1986. *Altruistic Emotion, Cognition, and Behavior.* Hillsdale, NJ: Erlbaum.

Eisenberg, N. 1992. *The Caring Child.* Cambridge, MA: Harvard University Press.

Elkind, D. 1990. "Academic Pressures—Too Much, Too Soon: The Demise of Play." In *Children's Play and Learning: Perspectives on Policy Implications,* eds. E. Klugman & S. Smilansky, 3–17. New York: Teachers College Press.

Filippini, T. 1990. "Introduction to the Reggio Approach." Paper presented at the Annual Conference of the National Association for the Education of Young Children, Washington, DC.

Forman, G. 2002. "Constructivist Teaching." Presentation at the Conference of the Canadian Association for Young Children, in Montreal.

Forman, G., & F. Hill. 1980. *Constructive play: Applying Piaget in the preschool.* Monterey, CA: Brooks/Cole.

Gandini, L. 1993. "The Fundamentals of the Reggio Emilia Approach to Early Childhood Education." *Young Children* 49 (1): 4–8.

Gandini, L. 1998. Conference on the inspiration and interpretation of Reggio Emilia at Loyalist College, Belleville, ON, Canada.

Gandini, L. 2012. "History, Ideas, and Basic Principles: An Interview With Loris Malaguzzi." In *The Hundred Languages of Children: The Reggio Emilia Experience in Transformation, 3rd ed.,* eds. C. Edwards, L. Gandini, & G. Forman, 27–71. Santa Barbara, CA: Praeger.

Garvey, C. 1990. *Play.* 2nd ed. Cambridge, MA: Harvard University Press.

Giudici, C., C. Rinaldi, & M. Krechevsky, eds. 2001. *Making Learning Visible: Children as Individual and Group Learners.* Reggio Emilia, Italy: Reggio Children; Cambridge, MA: Project Zero.

Gleick, J. 1987. *Chaos: Making a New Science.* New York: Penguin.

Gold, D., & M. Reiss. 1982. "Male Teacher Effects on Young Children: A Theoretical and Empirical Consideration." *Sex Roles* 8 (5): 493–513.

Goleman, D. 2006. *Social Intelligence: Beyond IQ, Beyond Emotional Intelligence.* New York: Bantam Books.

Gordon, M. 2005. *The Roots of Empathy: Changing the World Child by Child.* New York: The Experiment.

Grulovic, T. 2013. "From Coach to Full-Time Owner of His Own (Luxury) Team." *Globe and Mail,* May 11.

Hall, E. 2010. "Identity and Young Children's Drawings: Power, Agency, Control and Transformation." In *Play and Learning in the Early Years,* eds. P. Broadhead, J. Howard, & E. Wood, 95–112. London: Sage.

Hendrick, J., ed. 1997. *First Steps Toward Teaching the Reggio Way.* Upper Saddle River, NJ: Prentice Hall.

Hendrick, J., & P. Weissman. 2010. *Total Learning: Developmental Curriculum for the Young Child.* 8th ed. Upper Saddle River, NJ: Prentice Hall.

Hoffman, M.L. 2000. *Empathy and Moral Development: Implications for Caring and Justice.* Cambridge, United Kingdom: Cambridge University Press.

Hohmann, M., D. Weikart, & A.S. Epstein. 2008. 1995. *Educating Young Children: Active Learning Practices for Preschool and Child Care Programs.* 3rd ed. Ypsilanti, MI: High/Scope Press.

Hopkins, A.R. 2002. "Children and Grief: The Role of the Early Childhood Educator." *Young Children* 57 (1): 40–47.

Isaacs, S. [1930] 1968. *Intellectual Growth in Young Children.* New York: Schocken.

Jones, E. 2012. "The Emergence of Emergent Curriculum." *Young Children* 67 (2): 66–68.

Jones, E., & R.M. Cooper. 2006. *Playing to Get Smart.* New York: Teachers College Press.

Jones, E., & J. Nimmo. 1994. *Emergent Curriculum.* Washington, DC: NAEYC.

Katz, L.G., & S.C. Chard. 2000. *Engaging Children's Minds: The Project Approach.* 2nd ed. Stamford, CT: Ablex.

Khattar, R. 2009. "Pedagogy of Complex Relationality: Exploring Complexity Theory, Neurophenom-enology, and Attentiveness in Education." Unpublished doctoral dissertation, Faculty of Education, York University, Toronto.

Khattar, R., & C.A. Wien. 2012. "Illness and the Concept of Aesthetic Responsiveness in Early Child-hood Education." *Journal of the Canadian Association for Curriculum Studies* 10 (2): 70–91.

Kocher, L. 2010. "Families and Pedagogical Narration: Disrupting Traditional Understandings of Fam-ily Involvement." In *Flows, Rhythms, and Intensities of Early Childhood Education Curriculum*, ed. V. Pacini-Ketchabaw, 177–201. New York: Peter Lang.

Kohlberg, L. 1969. "Stage and Sequence: The Cognitive-Developmental Approach to Socialization." *Handbook of Socialization Theory and Research*, ed. D.A. Goslin, 347–480. Chicago: Rand McNally.

Kritchevsky, S., & E. Prescott. 1977. *Planning Environments for Young Children: Physical Space*. 2nd ed. Washington, DC: NAEYC.

Levin, D.E., & N. Carlsson-Paige. 2005. *The War Play Dilemma: What Every Parent and Teacher Needs to Know*. 2nd ed. New York: Teachers College Press.

Malaguzzi, L., 1998. "History, Ideas, and Basic Philosophy: An Interview With Lella Gandini." In *The Hundred Languages of Children: The Reggio Emilia Approach to Early Childhood Education— Advanced Reflections*, 2nd ed., eds. C. Edwards, L. Gandini, & G. Forman, 49–97. Greenwich, CT: Ablex.

Marion, M. 2011. *Guidance of Young Children*. 8th ed. Upper Saddle River, NJ: Pearson.

McMullen, M.B. 2010. "Confronting the Baby Blues: A Social Constructivist Reflects on Time Spent in a Behaviorist Infant Classroom." *Early Childhood Research and Practice* 12 (1) http://ecrp.uiuc.edu/v12n1/mcmullen.html.

McMullen, M.B., J.M. Addleman, A.M. Fulford, S.L. Moore, S.J. Mooney, S.S. Sisk, & J. Zachariah. 2009. "Learning to Be Me While Coming to Understand We: Encouraging Prosocial Babies in Group Settings." *Young Children* 64 (4): 20–28.

Montessori, M. [1912] 1964. *The Montessori Method*. New York: Schocken.

Montessori, M. [1949] 1969. *The Absorbent Mind*. New York: Schocken.

Moss, P. 2007. "Bringing Politics Into the Nursery: Early Childhood Education as a Democratic Process." Working Paper 43. The Hague, The Netherlands: Bernard van Leer Foundation. www.bernardvanleer.org/Bringing_politics_into_the_nursery_Early_childhood_education_as_a_democratic_practice.

Moss, P. 2012. "Micro-Project and Macro-Policy: Learning Through Relationships." In *The Hundred Languages of Children: The Reggio Emilia Experience in Transformation*, 3rd ed., eds. C. Edwards, L. Gandini, & G. Forman, 101–13. Santa Barbara, CA: Praeger.

Noddings, N. 2003. *Caring: A Feminine Approach to Ethics and Moral Education*. 2nd ed. Berkeley: University of California Press.

Olsson, L. 2009. *Movement and Experimentation in Young Children's Learning: Deleuze and Guattari in Early Childhood Education*. New York: Taylor & Francis.

Pacini-Ketchabaw, V., F. Nxumalo, L. Kocher, E. Elliott, & A. Sanchez. Forthcoming. *Journeys: Complexifying Early Childhood Practices Through Pedagogical Narration*. Toronto: University of Toronto Press.

Paley, V.G. 1986. *Boys and Girls: Superheroes in the Doll Corner*. Chicago: University of Chicago Press.

Paley, V.G. 2005. *A Child's Work: The Importance of Fantasy*. Chicago: University of Chicago Press.

Piaget, J. [1932] 1965. *The Moral Judgment of the Child*. New York: The Free Press.

Piccinini, S., & C. Giudici. 2012. "Reggio Emilia: A Transforming City." In *The Hundred Languages of Children: The Reggio Emilia Experience in Transformation*, 3rd ed., eds. C. Edwards, L. Gandini, & G. Forman, 89–99. Santa Barbara, CA: Praeger.

Pinar, W. 2008. *What Is Curriculum Theory?* New York: Routledge.

Polanyi, M. [1966] 2009. *The Tacit Dimension*. Chicago: University of Chicago Press.

Rinaldi, C. 1996. "Malaguzzi and the Teachers." *Innovations in Early Education: The International Reggio Exchange* 3 (4): 1.

Rinaldi, C. 2006. *In Dialogue With Reggio Emilia: Listening, Researching and Learning*. New York: Routledge.

Schön, D. 1983. *The Reflective Practitioner: How Professionals Think in Action*. New York: Basic Books.

Schön, D. 1987. *Educating the Reflective Practitioner: Toward a New Design for Teaching and Learning in the Professions*. San Francisco: Jossey-Bass.

Sellar, S. 2009. "The Responsible Uncertainty of Pedagogy." *Discourse: Studies in the Cultural Politics of Education* 30 (3): 347–60.

Shanker, S. 2013. *Calm, Alert, and Learning: Classroom Strategies for Self-Regulation*. Toronto: Pearson.

Shears, J. 2010. "Benefits of a Male's Presence in the Classroom." *National Head Start Association Dialog* 13 (1): 66–70.

Slaughter, V. 2005. "Young Children's Understanding of Death." *Australian Psychologist* 40 (3): 179–86.

Sokal, L., H. Katz, A. Sych-Yereniuk, L. Chochinov-Harder, M. Adkins, T. Grills, C. Stewart, & G. Priddle. 2005. *Male Reading Teachers: Effects on Inner-City Boys.* Winnipeg, MB, Canada: University of Manitoba/Winnipeg Inner City Research Alliance.

Sood, A.B., A. Razdan, E.B. Weller, & R.A. Weller. 2006. "Children's Reactions to Parental and Sibling Death." *Current Psychiatry Reports* 8 (2): 115–20.

Speece, M., & S. Brent. 1984. "Children's Understanding of Death: A Review of Three Components of a Death Concept." *Child Development* 55: 1671–86.

Sroufe, L.A. 1996. *Emotional Development: The Organization of Emotional Life in the Early Years.* Cambridge, United Kingdom: Cambridge University Press.

Stacey, S. 2009. *Emergent Curriculum in Early Childhood Settings.* St. Paul, MN: Redleaf Press.

Steele, B. 1998. *Draw Me a Story: An Illustrated Exploration of Drawing as Language.* Winnipeg, MB, Canada: Peguis.

Sumsion, J. 2005. "Male Teachers in Early Childhood Education: Issues and Case Study." *Early Childhood Research Quarterly* 20 (1): 109–23.

Tamminen, W. 2013. "School as a Living Organism." Unpublished paper, York University.

Thomas, N. 2008. "Small Boxes, Big Sound: Spontaneous Music in Kindergarten." In *Emergent Curriculum in the Primary Classroom: Interpreting the Reggio Emilia Approach in Schools*, ed. C.A. Wien, 19–25. New York: Teachers College Press; Washington, DC: NAEYC.

Toffler, A. 1981. *The Third Wave.* New York: Bantam Books.

Trungpa, C. 1987. *Shambhala: The Sacred Path of the Warrior.* Boston: Shambhala Books.

Vecchi, V. 1998. "The Role of the Atelierista." In *The Hundred Languages of Children: The Reggio Emilia Approach—Advanced Reflections*, 2nd ed., eds. C. Edwards, L. Gandini, & G. Forman, 139–47. Greenwich and Westport, CT: Ablex.

Vecchi, V. 2002. *Theater Curtain.* Reggio Emilia, Italy: Reggio Children.

Vecchi, V. 2010. *Art and Creativity in Reggio Emilia: Exploring the Role and Potential of Ateliers in Early Childhood Education.* New York: Routledge.

Vecchi, V., I. Cavallini, T. Filippini, & L. Trancossi, eds. 2011. *The Wonder of Learning: The Hundred Languages of Children.* Catalog to the Exhibit. Reggio Emilia, Italy: Reggio Children.

Vianello, R., & M.L. Marin. 1989. "Children's Understanding of Death." *Early Childhood Development and Care* 46: 97–104.

Vygotsky, L. 1976. "The Role of Play in Development." In *Play—Its Role in Development and Evolution,* eds. J. Bruner, A. Jolly, & K. Sylva. New York: Penguin.

Vygotsky, L.S. [1930–1935] 1978. *Mind in Society: The Development of Higher Psychological Processes,* eds. and trans. M. Cole, V. John-Steiner, S. Scribner, & E. Souberman. Cambridge, MA: Harvard University Press.

Waechter, E.H. 1984. "Dying Children: Patterns of Coping." In *Childhood and Death,* eds. H. Wass & C.A. Corr, 51–68. Washington, DC: Hemisphere.

Wien, C.A. 1995. *Developmentally Appropriate Practice in "Real Life": Stories of Teacher Practical Knowledge.* New York: Teachers College Press.

Wien, C.A. 1996. "Time, Work, and Developmentally Appropriate Practice." *Early Childhood Research Quarterly* 11: 377–403.

Wien, C.A. 1997. "A Canadian in Reggio Emilia: The 1997 Study Tour." *Canadian Children* 22 (2): 30–38.

Wien, C.A., ed. 2008. *Emergent Curriculum in the Primary Classroom: Interpreting the Reggio Emilia Approach in Schools.* New York: Teachers College Press; Washington, DC: NAEYC.

Wien, C.A., V. Guyevskey, & N. Berdoussis. 2011. "Learning to Document in Reggio-Inspired Education." *Early Childhood Research and Practice* 2.

Willis, C. 2002. "The Grieving Process in Children: Strategies for Understanding, Educating, and Reconciling Children's Perceptions of Death." *Early Childhood Education Journal* 29 (4): 221–26.

Willis, S. 2000. "The Impact of Noise in the Child Care Classroom." *Connections* 4 (1): 1–2.

Winnicott, D. [1971] 2005. *Playing and Reality.* 2nd ed. New York: Routledge.

Acknowledgments

There is something beautiful in working with others to create—whether it be educators working with children and families, or writers working with editors and designers. I was delighted by editor Derry Koralek's suggestion that my articles for *Young Children* be gathered together into a book, and have much appreciation for her detailed and careful attentiveness to this project and for her approachability and commitment: She can see from the tiniest details to the overarching vision for early childhood education. There are others behind the scenes who have been most helpful and whose efforts I also appreciate, in particular editors Elizabeth Wegner, Bry Pollack, Kathy Charner, and Amy Shillady, and designers Malini Dominey and Eddie Malstrom.

To my colleagues and dear friends who have participated in various ways in this book I offer my profound gratitude and affection. I cherish each for the depth of commitment and contribution they bring to our field of early childhood education, and for the hope they give to others for what we might yet create as a loving society that values its children. One group of these colleagues is those who have written reflections that follow the chapters: I am most grateful for their interest and for their voices, which form a sort of choral support for the work that is described. My partnership with a few of those writing reflections is new, and I especially appreciate the willingness of Mary Benson McMullen, Travis Wright, and Marian Marion to step into the landscape created and offer responses. Others are colleagues whose friendship and thinking I have valued for many years, and I thank Laurie Kocher and Veronica Pacini-Ketchabow, Margie Carter and Deb Curtis for our ongoing exchanges. Still others were important when I first entered the field as a fledgling author: Elizabeth Jones and Carol Copple offered support as I was stepping into an academic role, and their response to my work encouraged me to continue. Lella Gandini, with her warmth and graciousness, brings hope to many for the work we might do, and Carolyn Pope Edwards offers gifts of intellectual acuity and integrity. And to have our beloved Canadian colleague Sue Fraser within these pages is a blessing. Amy Dombro's scene-setting foreword arose from thoughtful and vibrant conversational exchange, and I thank her.

Another group of colleagues is all those with whom these chapters were written—my dear and gifted colleagues and friends Karyn Callaghan and Susan Stacey, and my former graduate student Valerie Quann. Nidia Sharma, another graduate student, assisted with literature reviews for the final two chapters and I am grateful for her work. The main actors with whom these chapters were written are, of course, the staff at Peter Green Hall Children's Centre who have collaborated with me on many occasions to investigate and interpret their practice and its development over time. It is almost 20 years we have worked together and I offer them and the children my deepest thanks, especially Barbara Bigelow and Bobbi-Lynn Keating.

Our collective debt to the educators of Reggio Emilia who have inspired us knows no bounds. They are a constant presence before us with the profound inspiration of what they have created in their city, the processes of engagement and political participation they encourage, and the marvelous expansiveness and depth of their vision for children in society. I am especially grateful for the efforts of Carla Rinaldi, Lella Gandini, and Amelia Gambetti, who have spent so much time with us in North America, supporting us in understanding their experience of early childhood education in Reggio Emilia.

Every person contributing to this book has been, for me, a beautiful colleague, someone from whose interest, engagement, intelligence, and attention I gained strength, conviction, and a sense of value as a participant in our field of early childhood education. I thank you.

About the Author

Carol Anne Wien, PhD, is a professor in the Faculty of Education at York University (in Toronto) and long-time friend and mentor to Peter Green Hall Children's Centre (in Halifax, Nova Scotia, Canada). She is the author of many articles and several books, including *Negotiating Standards in the Primary Classroom: The Teacher's Dilemma* (Teachers College Press, 2004) and *Developmentally Appropriate Practice in "Real Life": Stories of Teacher Practical Knowledge* (Teachers College Press, 1995), and editor of *Emergent Curriculum in the Primary Classroom: Interpreting the Reggio Emilia Approach in Schools* (Teachers College Press/NAEYC, 2008). She has been a long-time supporter of emergent curriculum and Reggio Emilia–inspired pedagogy in Canada, with particular interest in teacher development and the promise of emergent curriculum.

About the Contributors

Barbara Bigelow recently marked her 30th anniversary at Peter Green Hall Children's Centre. She has been the executive director since 1990.

Karyn Callaghan, MEd, is a professor of early childhood education at Charles Sturt University (Burlington, Ontario) and originator/coordinator of the Artists at the Centre project, which brings artists to centers exploring the Reggio Emilia approach.

Heather Cameron is a primary caregiver for infants at Peter Green Hall Children's Centre, where she has worked for 17 years and continues to be passionate about her work.

Annette Comeau is the director at Jubilee Road Children's Centre, Halifax, Nova Scotia. She has worked in the field of early learning and child care for the past 16 years.

Bobbi-Lynn Keating is the assistant director at Peter Green Hall Children's Centre. She has worked in the field of early learning and care for 24 years, 19 of which have been at Peter Green Hall. Bobbi was the recipient of the Prime Ministers Award for Excellence in Early Learning and Care in 2008.

Valerie Quann has an MEd from York University and has worked with children of all ages. She currently teaches in the early childhood education program at Seneca College in Toronto.

Joelle Deyarmond Rowlings is director of Leeds St. Childcare Centre and a part-time instructor at Nova Scotia College of Early Childhood Education. Formerly, she taught at Peter Green Hall Children's Centre.

Matthew Sampson works in the school-age program at Peter Green Hall Children's Centre. Matthew has worked in the field of early learning and care for 13 years. He has been at Peter Green Hall for the past 9 years. Matthew was the ECLC Award for Practice recipient in 2011.

Susan Stacey has worked in the field of early childhood education for more than 30 years, as an early childhood educator, director, practicum supervisor, and college instructor. She is the author of *Emergent Curriculum in Early Childhood Settings* (2009) and *Unscripted: Emergent Curriculum in Action* (2011), both published by Redleaf Press.

Justin West is a preschool room teacher and inclusion consultant at Peter Green Hall Children's Centre. Justin has worked in the field of early learning and care for 13 years, the last 7 at Peter Green Hall. Currently completing his Masters of Art Education at Boston University, Justin infuses creative expression into all the experiences at Peter Green Hall.